Who Will Stop the Bomb?

Who Will Stop the Bomb?
A Primer on Nuclear Proliferation

Roger Molander and Robbie Nichols
Roosevelt Center for American Policy Studies

Facts On File Publications
New York, New York • Oxford, England

From us born on the cusp of the nuclear age to all the kids born in the thick of it, in the hope we can pass on a world they can live with and a problem they can work.

Who Will Stop the Bomb? A Primer on Nuclear Proliferation

Copyright © 1985 by the Roosevelt Center for American Policy Studies

Library of Congress Cataloging in Publication Data

Molander, Roger C.
  Who will stop the bomb?

  Bibliography: p.
  1. Nuclear weapons. 2. Arms race--History--20th century. I. Nichols, Robbie. II. Title.
U264.M65 1985   327.1'74   85-10362
ISBN 0-8160-1283-0

Printed in the United States of America
10 9 8 7 6 5 4 3 2 1

CONTENTS

PREFACE

Say the words "nuclear arms race" and what comes to mind? For most people it is the 50,000 nuclear bombs the world is bristling with and the dismal state of relations between the two countries that own most of them, the harsh rhetoric with which both sides consign each other to the dustbin of history. This U.S.-Soviet doomsday machine is real enough. It's the only one big enough to threaten the earth, a fact not lost on its owners, who are forced to be careful about threatening to use it, rhetoric aside.

But there is a second arms race, masked by the big one, that is becoming even more dangerous--to Americans, Soviets, and the planet--than the superpowers' arms race. Just think ahead fifteen or twenty years and imagine what countries might have the bomb. Will the doctrine of deterrence, the mutual balance of terror, that keeps the U.S. and the Soviet Union from pushing the button still hold with this new set of players?

Assuming for a moment that the Americans and the Soviets are able to make deterrence work, who is more likely than either of them to vaporize a city in the coming decades? Well, look at the ten-most-want-it list: India, Israel, South Africa, Pakistan, Argentina, Brazil, Iraq, Libya, South Korea, and Taiwan. There are names on that list to conjure terror not just in Moscow and Washington but in other national capitals as well--particularly when they recognize that a suitcase, or a pickup truck, could be the delivery vehicle.

And then there's a third arms race more hidden than the second one. The third can't even properly be called a race. "Race" implies a competition, with counting and rationality and some sense of order. Those nation-states that have the bomb got it to ensure their security. But the players in this third arms race--terrorists or madmen--do not even fit our categories of thought about security: They have no borders to secure.

Will deterrence work at all for outlaw nations or terrorist gangs or madmen who have no stake in the status quo? What could possibly deter them? The concept of deterrence rests on the fear of retaliation, but there are no fingerprints on the bomb. There is no defense against a person willing to die in order to destroy Washington or Moscow or Tehran or Tel Aviv. Our only hope is to keep such people from getting the bomb in the first place.

Listening to the hostile rhetoric flying back and forth between the superpowers, it is hard to believe that they share some common ground. But proliferation is a common danger. How much good will all their nuclear bean-counting have been if one day Washington or Moscow just disappears by an unknown hand? Careful attention to controlling the U.S.-Soviet nuclear arms race may save us from the holocaust they could visit on the earth, but it does nothing to stay the hands of terrorists or renegade nations--especially those that might think the world a better place without *both* capitals.

Proliferation is a weighty word, but that word has to get out. The average man or woman may know enough about the subject to be justly afraid of Libya's Colonel Qaddafi or Iran's Ayatollah Khomeini getting the bomb. But seeing the problem whole and thinking about ways to contain it are hard to do. The subject doesn't play well in the news and barely surfaced in the 1984 U.S. presidential election campaign. News dribbles out--material missing from a nuclear power plant one day, heavy water shipped to Argentina another, an unwritten deal with China the next--and all these "minor" stories sink beneath the weight of the major crises which grab the headlines and lead the television news. Meanwhile, the slow and seemingly inexorable leaking of know-how and wherewithal continues.

In the prologue of this book we have imagined a future in which the countries that have the bomb have managed to make the world safer--or so they thought. Then one summer night in 1996, Washington disappears. Hiroshima, Nagasaki, Washington, D.C....

As you will learn in reading this book, the trends point toward a world full of nuclear weapons--a world wherein anyone who wants the bomb can get it. The effort to control the spread of nuclear weapons just isn't working--or at least not working well enough to halt the process rather than merely slowing it down. Can dramatic changes in course prevent the sobering world we have imagined from coming into being? What can we do about it? What can you do about it?

This book wrestles with those questions. It intends to give average citizens--the man or woman in the street--the same kind of background material and options that the President of the United States gets from his national security advisors, only written in English "that even cats and dogs can read," rather than technical jargon. It intends to persuade them, as citizens of a democracy, to demand that their nation commit its considerable energies to an attempt to stem the tide of nuclear proliferation while there is still time. And that means now. Nobody said it better than Daniel Webster, in words that are still valid after all these years:

Nothing will ruin the country if the people themselves undertake its safety, and nothing can save it if they leave that safety in any hands but their own.

When you finish this book, you will probably know as much about the problems posed by nuclear proliferation as the President of the United States does. We hope you will think long and hard about what the recognition of this danger demands of you--and of all of us as a people and as a species. We hope that you will use your knowledge to act, with effect, so that the image we present of 1996 never comes to pass.

Roger Molander
Robbie Nichols
Washington, D.C.
March, 1985

ACKNOWLEDGMENTS

We would like to acknowledge the many hands and skills that helped make this book: Leonard S. Spector, who reviewed the last draft for accuracy and whose book *Nuclear Proliferation Today* and Roosevelt Center manuscript *The Other Nuclear Arms Race* supplied many of the facts used in Chapters Five and Six; William Metz, who fixed technological glitches in Chapter Two; Carole Jacobs, who designed the book's architecture and wrote the first draft for Chapter Three; Lise Hartman, who prepared the first draft outline for the forums considered in Chapter Seven; Larry Smith, who crafted the concept "first arms race, second arms race, third arms race"; and a host of reviewers who gave us their good counsel.

A NOTE ABOUT
THE ROOSEVELT CENTER

This book is the first in a series of policy primers to be produced by the Roosevelt Center for American Policy Studies. The Roosevelt Center is a nonprofit, nonpartisan, public policy research institute with offices in Washington, D.C., and Chicago, Illinois. Its goals are to clarify the policy choices before the nation and to encourage and facilitate the participation of citizens in the decision-making process at all levels of government. Founded in 1982, the Roosevelt Center takes its name and inspiration from three Roosevelts--Theodore, Eleanor, and Franklin--who courageously addressed our nation's future and brought clarity to America's vision of itself.

PROLOGUE: AUGUST 6, 1996

I don't sleep much anymore, so I saw it. I didn't know it was Washington, but I knew it was the end.

I'm as old as the century and I've seen a lot of death. I worked in a field hospital in France in the Great War, before we knew to number them. I held dying boys after we had saved everybody we could. Near as I can tell, a mortar shell serves as well as a bomb, if you're close enough. Dying is always the end of the world for the one who's doing it. Nobody mouthed the old lie about how sweet and fitting it is to die for your country. They mostly cried out for their mothers or sweethearts.

The Second World War was *about* something. Pearl Harbor. Those pictures from the death camps. You can divide your life into the time before you saw them and the time after. As you can with Hiroshima. People still aren't sure what the first one was about. And *no* one knows what this is about. Or who killed Washington. Or whether it's over yet.

I was on the porch watching the stars when the flash came. Like the lightning that hit my window when I was a child: it didn't light things, it *was* light. Everything drowned in it. A great blow knocked me off the step. The very air was roaring. When I could see again, the whole sky was violet. I crouched in the lilac bushes, waiting for the rest, but there wasn't any more. I was there a long time.

And I knew it had to be Washington. It was about far enough away. I knew I should get up and go inside, what with still being alive and all. But there just didn't seem any point. I have to admit I was glad the wind was south-southwest. I've read all the manuals about fallout and running and hiding, but I didn't want to move. And I didn't want to see the image on the other side of the house.

The lilac bushes seemed like the place to stay. I've been watching wars now for eighty years. And I couldn't tell if this was one. It seemed like something worse. People in Japan probably thought so too if they were far enough away to think. I could never understand the second bomb, not three days later. I'd really like to

1

think up a reason for Nagasaki--something besides ignorance and rage--that didn't make me fear for the species. It was easier than thinking about Washington. And whether there would be more bombs.

I was in Washington once in the middle fifties when I went up to visit a friend in trouble. I don't remember much except that walking some places you felt like you were in the eighteenth century. It was almost as good as hearing Mozart, and I thought how lucky we were to have got those declarative sentences from the flower of the eighteenth century. I went to visit those sentences, and found the Declaration of Independence an even more moving memorial to Jefferson than the marble building. The words carved on the wall will serve, but I prefer the document whole.

My friend worked at the National Archives and one day I was there at quitting time. The Declaration of Independence and the Constitution were lowered into a fifty-ton vault, where they spend every night safe from acts of God or man. Even then, it seemed an ominous ritual, nothing like lowering the flag. They're probably safe there even now. But will they survive this night as something more than parchment? I can't think about the people.

Who could have done this? Hard to imagine that it's the Russians. We're not at war. We're not even close; it's nothing like the old days. They seemed to learn as much from Afghanistan as we did from Vietnam. It takes a lot longer if you don't have a free press. It took long enough here. But enough bitter experience and the word gets out. There are wars not worth the cost, and we both seem to have figured out that the last one worth it was World War II.

It's hard to imagine we might ever be allies again, if we ever were. The enemy of my enemy is my friend was more like it, and it took a while to get there. It wasn't true in 1939 when they carved up Poland with Hitler and took over the Baltic states. We probably didn't look much like allies to them either a few years later when they were desperate for us to invade Europe to take the heat off the Eastern Front. But we finally did invade at Normandy, and together we won the war. I don't think they'd attack us now. But who would? And what do they hope to get from us?

I thought a long time about who did it. And if it would stop here if we found out who did it. Strange, but it made me hope we never find out--if it stops.

Just before dawn, I heard some people calling my name. They were my neighbors, who left Washington for the Blue Ridge five years ago because they thought it was a better place for their children, a girl twelve, and a boy about seven. Quality of life, they were looking for. I don't know them well, but what does pass between us is real-- especially the girl. I'm a solitary soul, and it had been years since anyone touched me as that child did, does.

The girl came around the corner of the porch and helped me get up. I'd been crouched in the bushes a long time and my bones are old. When we rounded the porch you could see north. There was a roiling black cloud hanging there in the early light. The girl asked me if Washington was still burning and when it would go out. I told her soon, they'll stop it. Fire engines and all. We know how to fight fires. Privately, I wondered how far it had got. It has been a dry summer. Where's the natural limit, especially to the north, if it's a big enough fire with no one fighting it?

We all went inside and the woman and I got breakfast. It was good to have something to do. The coffee smelled as good as it always does, like nothing had changed. The man sat on a bench with an arm around either child.

When the flash came, they had huddled in a bedroom, waiting for the end. After a while, when there weren't any more bombs, they had turned on the television. So they knew a lot.

The boy talked the whole time. The mushroom cloud was just like the pictures, only it moved and lit up with lightning crackling inside it. What was left? How about the Air and Space Museum? Couldn't they fix it? The zoo? The Capitol? We all looked at each other. Nobody wanted to tell him. After a while, he fell silent and climbed into his mother's lap. It'll be all right, we tell them after a bad dream. But if it comes true, what do you say then?

We didn't even know what to say to each other. We had thought the world was safer than this. We weren't friends with the Russians and neither of us was friends with the Islamic Kingdom. But now that the world is armed to the teeth, we can see you don't have to be friends to have relations. Not if the other choice is extinction. In fact, the only real war on right now is a tribal one in Central Africa. It's an uneasy peace. But nobody wants to break it. So who did? Who could slaughter a city when there's not even a war on? And if one, why not two? Why not ten?

The woman said the cloud was near Baltimore and moving up the eastern seaboard unless the wind shifted. People couldn't get out very fast. There was a ragged column walking north out of the ruined city, carrying what they could. Some were wearing makeshift bandages and even splints. They were eerily quiet, dazed, like sleepwalkers. There were grocery carts and golf carts and baby buggies piled high. What one thing do you save from a burning house--or city? One man was carrying a painting, stopping every few yards to redistribute the load. A girl carrying a rabbit filled the screen for a moment, and then it cut back to the whole throng. A good many were carrying their children and could carry nothing else. The reporter came on and said they weren't showing any badly injured people, that it was important not to panic. He showed a map of where the cloud was expected to go and how much time people had to get out. And what those who couldn't move should do.

The man said the president was killed, and the cabinet, the Supreme Court, the Joint Chiefs of Staff, and all but a couple dozen Senators and Congressmen. Nobody knows who is president now.

He said the chain of command that usually makes decisions in Washington is gone. NORAD headquarters in Cheyenne Mountain in Colorado is calling the shots, he said. All submarines have been put to sea and the bombers dispersed. They're still waiting, like the rest of us. What will happen next? Who's in charge? No one knows.

The children had fallen asleep, the boy in his mother's lap and the girl with her head on the table. So we talked about what to do. They want to head farther into the hills, visit his sister in West Virginia, and they asked me to come along. I was glad for the offer, but I don't want to move. They roused the children and went to pack the car.

I wanted to know what was happening, but my radio was

broken. Had been for a long time. I never bothered to get it fixed because I have a short-wave radio. It's fifty years old, but it still works. I listen to England and France and Germany in the middle of the night. I like sharing somebody else's daytime while the whole countryside is asleep. But the only thing I could get at the moment was static.

A little later they stopped to say goodbye, and left me their television. The girl gave me a bunch of Queen Anne's lace she had picked on the roadside. They tried to leave food as well, but I wouldn't have it. I live on biscuits and sausage, and have plenty. And they might need it where they're going.

There was nothing to be done. I could hear bluejays fighting over the raspberries just outside the window. I usually beat them to it. This morning the birds can have them. It might be their last meal and they don't even know it. They're lucky not to know. It's been five hours now. Will there be more? Where will this end?

I turned on the television and flipped the channels. There were only two. The newsmen have aged since last night. It wasn't like most disasters, where they seem secretly pleased at having important things to say.

A government spokesman came on. He said the six living Senators were forming a tribunal that would run the government for now. According to the Constitution, they were supposed to elect a new head of the Senate who would then become president. But none of them wanted to do that. The Constitution hadn't allowed for only six being left. They were meeting as he spoke in an undisclosed place.

A man in uniform came on. Maryland and Virginia are under martial law and looters will be shot on sight. He cut to a military checkpoint where the Army has cordoned off the southern borders of what used to be Washington. He showed the Army and National Guard helping people get out in the north. He said we don't know who did this. The Russians and the Arabs say it wasn't them. It's clear they need to make the case.

The Soviet general secretary came on the screen. Unheard of. He said we must believe that Russia did not commit this outrage. That he was as appalled as the rest of the world. That he had dispatched doctors and medical supplies due to arrive in Norfolk late in the day. And

5

that no news of the death of Washington would be permitted in his country, in order to avoid panic.

The man in uniform came back on. He said that the bomb had not been airborne. That even something that comes in at treetop level was visible to the sophisticated radars that watched Washington. They think it was assembled in the city.

Every few minutes the same message came on. "Washington, D.C., was destroyed by a nuclear weapon at 3:07 a.m. this morning. All U.S. military forces are on alert. We know of no other nuclear weapon explosions here or elsewhere in the world. Do not panic. We do not expect further hostilities." And then something like a weather map tracking the cloud and where it was going and how fast. Can there still be people just getting up who don't know it yet? What will happen when everybody knows?

I couldn't watch anymore so I went outside. There's a meadow nearby with a swing in it, one of those white lattice-work affairs with two seats facing each other. I don't sit in it often, because it has a limited number of swings left in it before it falls down. It's a relic and rickety, but it takes me back to a time worth remembering. Even if the world is to end, I want to remember the parts I love.

I was lost for a while in a time more real to me than this one, when bird cries brought me back. A wren was raising a great racket, perched on the opposite seat. A fearful assault indeed, but he backed up when he saw he had got my attention. There was a nest in a crevice above me, and I could see young ones, or rather three gaping beaks. The female flashed back and forth stuffing grubs into one mouth and then another, without giving me a glance. The male braved the swing again and made such a clatter that he dropped the worm he was carrying. He flitted from branch to fence post to parts of the swing, always with a great stream of threats, but he never delivered a single worm.

There's a division of work and feeling here that I want to understand, so I watched for a while. The female only wants to feed the young; she doesn't even deign to see me. The male wants to secure the perimeters. In fact, he can't get a mate if he doesn't command a territory.

And if he couldn't hold it, there wouldn't be enough grubs. There's some evolutionary advantage to aggression at small scales. In wrens it seems like the males' part of nurturance. I wonder if a female who ends up with a nest alone can make it?

At least birds don't kill their own kind. You have to be human to bring off mass slaughter. You have to be able to see the enemy as another species: the infidel is not quite human. But I thought humankind had got over the hump, that we had learned that we could disagree vehemently with each other's politics and religions and economics, but it was too dangerous to do anything to each other. The doomsday machine had lots of triggers and a fair number of shaky hands on them. We had to leave each other alone. Can we still? Depends on who did it. We might have been forced to see our enemies as human beings. But who is this enemy?

It was after midnight and I tried for the BBC. I could only get it in little pieces with bursts of static in between. Britain had airlifted its best burn units. They were already on the ground in Maryland. Estimates are a half million dead or dying. They had sent all the morphine and heroin they could. People are being triaged. I guess it's pretty easy to tell who will die anyway. I lost it in static then, so I turned the television back on.

The fire is still out of control, but the wind has shifted to the west. A satellite picture showed a great spreading blotch from far enough up to look abstract. They weren't showing any pictures from airplanes. But they said they were up there sampling the air. How will that tell who did it? And what will we do if we find out?

They cut to Los Angeles. Martial law's been declared in California too. There were shots from earlier in the day, all the freeways blocked with people trying to get out. It stretched nearly to the Sierras on all roads going east and only the front of the line was moving. They showed a grocery store that had been stripped to its bare shelves. The owner looked dazed: "They even took the floor wax," he said. There were lots of shots of the National Guard and the Army posted on the streets. And a whole encampment around a grocery distributor. They cut to Miami where there looked to be a riot on. I turned it

7

off.

I couldn't sleep, so I tried the radio again. The chancellor came on in Bonn and appealed to people to stay where they were. Refugees are pouring into Hamburg and Frankfurt from all the places near the eastern border. Be rational, he urged. The Soviets have promised to make no move in the face of this catastrophe. In fact, he said, the rumor has spread throughout Moscow and people are walking out. Though there has been no official announcement. When Beethoven came on the radio, they thought their general secretary had died. They couldn't keep the real disaster a secret even though they tried. I guess word travels fast by mouth if the secret is bad enough.

It seemed more important to know what was happening here, so I turned the television back on. The network said it would broadcast 24 hours a day until further notice. That it's running on a skeleton staff.

There are rumors of threats against New York City. The mayor came on and said not to worry. "Look, there were four calls, from the sort of folks who think they're getting messages from their bridgework. They clearly don't have both oars in the water. We hung on to them long enough to trace the calls and all four are in custody at this moment."

There were shots of New York from a helicopter. The jams getting out were endless. Nobody was moving. The mayor came on again and urged people to stay. "You can't leave anyway unless you walk," he said. "We must stand firm. This is not a war. We don't think there will be any more bombs."

The general secretary came on again. He was standing in Red Square in the afternoon sun with some other old men, the Politburo I guess. "We are showing our innocence," he said. "I am standing in Red Square. Would I stay here if I had left a bomb in Washington? Would I be going to Geneva this afternoon for a meeting with the NATO ministers and the Chinese premier?"

The reporter came back on and said Moscow is emptying out. The Red Army is supposed to contain it, but people are still getting out. Some troops are deserting to go with their families. But nobody's got shot yet. The fear is real enough. If Washington, by an unknown hand, why not Moscow? I suppose even to the Red Army shooting people seems redundant if the whole city might go.

The program cut to a group of Arab ministers in Damascus. A defense minister spoke for them. He wanted to disavow an earlier report about a mullah in Iran who called this the judgment of Allah on Washington. That was a great libel on Allah. He might have used swords in the past, like Jehovah and the Christian God, but he does not use nuclear weapons. He was sorry for the strain of hatred running through the more fundamentalist parts of the Islamic world, but he wanted to assure us it was under control.

The reporter came on again and said the Pope had just arrived at a candlelight vigil in Central Park. It's 1:00 a.m., but a great mass of people is still gathered there. It was moving to see the people who stayed. I can understand loving a place that much. The Pope came on the screen. Christ's vicar on Earth. Here to show his identity with suffering humanity. He makes an appeal to whoever did it. It's the first time I realized that whoever did it is probably watching. Unless they went with Washington. Nothing can be worth this, he said. No rage can be this great. There can be no cause for the slaughter of innocents. He even called on Americans not to answer in kind if they find out who did it. The whole world must try to stop it here, he said. If we unleashed this fury on anyone, it would be death even greater than Washington, it would consume our values as a people.

Then Chicago came on, with a man on the street in Old Town. The streets are full of people. Nobody wants to be at home alone, I guess. He went into a bar on State Street. People were watching television and drinking and it was very quiet. A few couples were dancing.

Then the scene cut to one of those new places where the young folks gather. It was loud and everyone was dancing. It seemed faintly inhuman to me, like dancing on the Titanic while it went down. But it's clear these young people get something from their music, probably what I get from Mozart. Music is another world and for as long as it lasts you don't have to live in this one. This though was full of primal noises and disorder and mating cries. Tonight it seems an apt reflection of the world.

I haven't slept for two days, so I turned off the television and made myself a whiskey and hot water. But

I couldn't stop thinking.

Secretaries of War wanted to win. The last one I remember was Henry Stimson during World War II, and he did. Sometime after the bomb all the ministers of war got to be ministers of defense. Right when it got impossible to defend things. They argued about what it would mean to win and if anybody could do it. Along the lines of if there's a nuclear war and afterwards we've got 30 days of wheat left to eat and they have 31 days' worth left, they won.

It was mostly the people who saw the wheat fields sown with missile silos. And that day 32 would follow as surely as the night. It was probably the news about nuclear winter that brought us to our senses, at least those of us with lots of bombs. Striking back didn't seem to matter if the earth would do it anyway. Even politicians figured out they'd be just as dead if it took thirty days instead of thirty minutes. Deader maybe, what with more time for everything human to come apart in the bitter darkness.

So it seemed like the world had got safer. Just in the last several years. It still looks like us and them, but we don't rattle missiles at each other like we used to. I think it was the Arab bomb that got our attention; made us see how many other people there are in the world, what a small slice are Russians and Americans. Slowly more and more countries were getting the bomb. It was piecemeal and hard to follow, for regular folks anyway. The stories were right there in the papers, I guess, for anybody who could connect the dots. But each test or revelation about a new country that could probably build the bomb was a terrible shock. And we sure didn't want all those other countries to act like us--or build arsenals like ours. So we and the Russians had finally begun cutting back. And nobody's even come close to using the bomb, nothing remotely like 1962--until now.

So who could have done it? Lots of countries have the bomb, but who would kill Washington, knowing that the earth might go with it?

The whiskey and water didn't help. I still couldn't sleep. So I turned the television back on.

The mayor of New York came on again. "Look, I was wrong. You should worry. Maybe you should get out. We got another call, at exactly 3:07 a.m. It only lasted 15 seconds. I've played it over and over again. We've got a battery of psychiatrists analyzing it. We don't know if it's real or not. But the man claimed he destroyed Washington and told us to look in a certain footlocker in Grand Central Station and he'd talk to us later. Then he hung up. This is what we found." And he held up a piece of what looked to be hardened scrambled eggs. Yellow-cake, he said it was, some uranium ore that can be made into bombs. "It's a long way from being a bomb," he said. "But it is a message of sorts. We don't know what it means. The man didn't threaten to destroy New York. We don't know if he's telling the truth, and, if he is, whether he has another bomb. And, if he does, whether he will use it. But you have to know. You have to make your own choice." The camera cut away a second too late and you could see his face crumple.

I've had enough. I don't want to know any more. I don't want to hear it or see it or think about it. And I particularly don't want to watch some politician cry. Why didn't they do something about it when they had a chance? What are they good for if they couldn't see this coming?

I took another whiskey and hot water out to the porch. It's been forty years since I had more than one, but this night is hard to get through. It was only last night. Funny how life seems so short when a day like this is endless. I'll be ninety-eight in ten days if the world lasts so long. I feel all right about leaving the world. I didn't know that it might leave me.

Not thinking about it is harder than I thought. But the cicadas help, and the whiskey. Maybe I can make a separate peace, if only for this night. The cicadas have managed it. The song is coming from everywhere at once. Somehow they all in concert take it up into great swells and then down into quiet passages. Praise for a summer night from a choir that doesn't know there's anything else. Imagine their seventeen years in the earth. No wonder this anthem breaks out when they do.

It seems I can sleep after all, here in this upright chair, with all the while this insistent drumming, like a mother's heartbeat or an ocean breaking on the shore.

1

NUCLEAR ANARCHY

Well, who did do it? If it happened, what would we ever find out? Within a few hours after the detonation we could have planes gathering air samples that would tell us something. After a time we could go into the dead zone that used to be Washington. We could get the hot pieces, tag the evidence, find ground zero. We could even trace the process backward from what was left, like an equation, and figure out what kind of bomb it was. Say it was a crude bomb made with uranium. What would that prove? If you can make an elegant bomb, you can also make a crude one and pass it off as the work of bumblers. So how would we ever find out who did it?

And even if we did, what could we do about it? Washington would be just as dead. Even vengeance might be impossible. What if it turned out to be the work of a small band of terrorists? Could we stomach destroying their country or even their hometown, if its only crime was giving them life? What if it turned out to be an American, home-grown madman with nothing to lose, a Charles Manson who somehow got his hands on the bomb?

And even more critical, once Washington was destroyed, where would it end? How could we contain the crisis? What if it were Moscow instead of Washington? Or Peking? Or New Delhi? Or Tel Aviv?

We can't answer these questions. But we must worry that, one day, sooner or later, the world will have to contend with such a threat. Even if we learn how to get along with the Russians--and with the rest of the nuclear-tipped world, which could number fifteen countries by the end of the century--nuclear weapons are here to stay. And so are terrorists and madmen. Can we even hope they won't find each other?

Imagine a world where instead of the computer revolution and the PC, there's a nuclear revolution and the PB--the personal bomb. Maybe dozens of them in private hands. Think for a moment about what sort of private hands it might fall into. The Mafia? A multinational corporation? A fanatic religious sect? Assorted psychotics? Fill in the blank with your worst nightmare. It could come true.

What could make anyone break the nuclear taboo that has held now for forty years? The most frightening prospect is an isolated psychopath acting alone. He wouldn't even need a second opinion. Take a mind fractured along religious fault lines. He might think his orders are coming from God (or Allah) and see himself as an instrument of divine justice. If he belonged to the Judeo-Christian tradition, he might see Western cities as Sodom and Gomorrah, full of wickedness, an abomination on the earth. Even the image of destruction in the biblical story might play into his madness: It's the wrath of God, but it looks for all the world to a modern eye like a nuclear explosion.

There *are* people this crazy. Every country breeds them. The only far-fetched part of this conjecture is how the fanatic would get the bomb. You'd have to assume he'd received advanced training in physics and engineering during a lucid interval, and that he was only mad north-northwest, like Hamlet: that when the wind was southerly he could summon the rationality to get the wherewithal to build a bomb. Or you could assume he'd had SWAT team training somewhere in his past, in which case he might be able to steal one.

Should you think it impossible for a single person to assemble a workable bomb, listen to Theodore Taylor, a former U.S. bomb designer: "One person working alone, who possessed about ten kilograms of plutonium oxide and a substantial amount of chemical explosive could, within several weeks, design and build a crude fission bomb using materials and equipment that could be purchased from a hardware store and from commercial suppliers of scientific equipment for student laboratories."

These assumptions are easier to credit if the number of actors grows. Group psychosis yields a larger number of hands and skills. It might also yield a motive more credible to the modern world, where politics is what religion was to the medieval world. Politics can also make men mad, and it seems a likelier spring to propel a group of would-be nuclear terrorists.

A small terrorist group would also be likelier than a

solitary madman to attempt the theft of a nuclear weapon or weapons material. Even in the United States, security at nuclear facilities can be breached. In September 1982, a U.S. "threat assessment" team made up of ex-Green Berets and SWAT team veterans staged a mock assault on the Savannah River plant that produces plutonium for U.S. nuclear weapons. The plant's guards reportedly responded 16 minutes *after* the assault team could have made off with enough plutonium for at least one atom bomb. There can be little assurance that nuclear installations in other parts of the world are better protected. And the statistical probability of a successful heist will increase with time and with the enormous growth in the amount of bomb material in circulation around the world.

There have been past models for such small terrorist groups--the Japanese Red Army, the Baader-Meinhof gang in Germany, the Red Brigade in Italy, the Symbionese Liberation Army or the Weather Underground in the United States. The wanton destruction of innocent life is the most frightening aspect of such groups. For them the taboo against killing innocents carries no weight. And though such groups have refrained from mass killing so far, it may be only that it doesn't yet serve their purposes. The taboo might not hold in the future. The gravest danger then would be the appearance of a nihilistic group, especially one possessing nuclear weapons.

In that case, the very breaking of such a powerful taboo might itself be an incitement. If terror is an end in itself, there is no better means than an atomic bomb. A group acting out of rage and alienation and a sense of powerlessness has no stake in preserving the status quo or any conceivable variation of it. Such persons might have no stake in life itself and may take a city with them in a spasm of suicidal rage. Again, the problem of getting the bomb seems insurmountable. But there have been mad scientists in this world, and a few of them acting together would suffice.

It won't be just America's problem. The Soviet Union has also made enemies who might not balk at nuclear threats for political ends. Here are two articles buried within pages of the *New York Times* from the summer of 1984. The terrorists here had only anti-tank rockets, and no one was killed. But listen to the passions expressed and project yourself into a future where nuclear weapons are widely available:

ROCKET FIRED IN BEIRUT STRIKES SOVIET EMBASSY

Special to the *New York Times*

BEIRUT, Lebanon, July 20. *The Soviet Embassy here was hit by a rocket tonight, causing damage but no casualties, the police said.*

It was the second attack on the Soviet diplomatic compound this year. In April rockets were fired at the Soviet cultural center.

In the attack tonight, a B-7 anti-tank rocket, a weapon commonly carried by many militiamen here, was fired at the fenced-off embassy on Cornish Maazra in a predominantly Moslem section of West Beirut.

Responsibility for the attack in April was claimed by the Islamic Holy War organization, which said it was in retaliation for Soviet policies in Afghanistan.

BEIRUT, July 20 (AP). *A male telephone caller told The Associated Press bureau in Beirut about an hour after the attack that it had been carried out by the Organization of the Sharp Sword, a group not heard of before. He said such attacks would continue unless the Russians stopped "interfering in Lebanese internal politics."*

The caller read a statement that said the attack was directed against the "Soviet espionage center."

The statement he read added, "The will which forced the Marines and French out of Beirut is capable of shaking the earth under the feet of the Russians."

The Organization of the Sharp Sword has spoken its first word. What will its last one be? Factions proliferating under the Islamic Holy War umbrella present a particular danger: They are driven by politics *and* religion. The two are one in fundamentalist parts of the Moslem world in a way that we who hold separation of church and state as a first principle can barely fathom. Extremist groups, like the Iranian members of Martyrs of the Islamic Revolution arrested in the summer of 1984 in Spain, even turn against fellow Moslems. This small terrorist cell was allegedly getting orders directly from Tehran and planning to attack a Saudi Arabian airliner.

Police seized grenade launchers, machine guns, explosives, and a good deal of Khomeini propaganda. In cases like this, it is clear that the categories terrorist and madman and nation--like religion and politics--are not mutually exclusive.

Listen to the Ayatollah himself, speaking in December 1984 on the occasion of Mohammed's birthday:

War is a blessing for the world and for all nations. It is God who incites men to fight and to kill. The Koran says: "Fight until all corruption and all rebellion have ceased." The wars the Prophet led against the infidels were a blessing for all humanity. Imagine that we soon win the war [against Iraq]. That will not be enough, for corruption and resistance to Islam will still exist. The Koran says: "War, war until victory...The mullahs with corrupt hearts who say that all this is contrary to the teachings of the Koran are unworthy of Islam. Thanks to God, our young people are now, to the limits of their means, putting God's commandments into action. They know that to kill the unbelievers is one of man's greatest missions.

The Pope sending Crusaders off to fight the Saracens might have spoken a blessing that would sound just as frightening to modern ears. But the Western world had its holy wars back when the limit of its means was the crossbow. How can the world survive a holy war if the limit rises to nuclear weapons?

Terrorist cells are on the rise in America too, though the violence they have committed is fairly limited. The same week that the Organization of the Sharp Sword made its first appearance, the *Wall Street Journal* featured American terrorist groups on its front page. The Black Liberation Army, the Weather Underground, and the FALN (an extremist splinter from the MLN, a law-abiding Puerto Rican independence group) got the most column inches, but the piece also noted 13 bombings over the past year and a half claimed by the United Freedom Front, the Armed Resistance Unit, and the Revolutionary Fighting Group.

Resurgent European urban guerillas are more deadly than their American counterparts, as witness the spate of killings and bombings in the winter of 1984-85 in Portugal, Spain, France, Belgium, and West Germany. "The new scourge of civilization" is how West German Chancellor Helmut Kohl characterized the alliance of the Red Army Faction (formerly the Baader-Meinhof gang) in West Germany with Direct Action in France and the Fighting Communist Cells in Belgium. Their announced goal is to "shake the imperialist system" through coordinated attacks on NATO installations and personnel. "Terrorism is the most efficient method of destabilizing a democracy," said former French Foreign Minister Claude Cheysson, noting the anxiety sowed by this revival of European terrorism. For now, the terrorists only have the store of conventional explosives they stole in Belgium last year. Imagine the extreme social disintegration if they even claimed to have a nuclear bomb and threatened to destroy an American base in Wiesbaden or Frankfurt.

The most frightening thing about these two categories --individual madmen or half-crazed terrorist groups--is that they don't respond to the sticks and carrots that make the rest of us behave. There is no way to buy them off.

The next larger category of concern--an independent political group big enough to have state-like impulses and state-like political ends, but capable of terrorist acts--might have a price. But it might be too high. Such a group could make extravagant threats even if it feared the repercussions of actually detonating a bomb: Nations that gave such a group aid and comfort might abandon it; Revolutionaries or factions in a civil war might not want to blow up a piece of earth they wanted, in time, to win; a nuclear explosion would cost popular support and legitimacy, "unacceptable damage" aside from destruction, and loss of lives. But the threat alone could be of enormous value.

What if the Black September faction of the PLO slipped a crude bomb into Tel Aviv and threatened to blow it up unless Israel abandoned the West Bank within 30 days? Or claimed to have atomic bombs in an American city or two and demanded an immediate end to U.S. military support of Israel? What would the president do? Refuse and hope it was a bluff? Give in to any demand, knowing that success in working their will would lead the terrorists to escalating demands? There are no good choices.

None of these groups or others that haven't surfaced

yet have got their hands on nuclear weapons, as far as we know. Maybe we can count on the continued strength of the global taboo against mass killing. And yet...if it is ever broken, even by a credible threat, think of the copycat possibilities. If a nuclear threat ever worked, it could become a fashion, perhaps within the reach of any terrorist group that had even a workable blueprint, whether or not they knew what to do with it; remember the wave of airline highjackings after the first one worked? It wasn't until the U.S. negotiated with Cuba in 1971 for an end to sanctuary for airline highjackers that this particular turn of terrorism abated.

All states with any stake in the status quo (and that's most of the 169 countries there are) have a common interest in keeping the bomb out of private hands, whatever they may decide about acquiring it for themselves. But states--or more precisely, governments--always seem to have more pressing problems and fail to see the handwriting on the wall.

States tend to plan mostly for the immediate future, the next five years or so--maybe ten years if they're somewhat more provident. We must do better than this with regard to nuclear proliferation. We must project ourselves along various paths ranging as far as twenty-five or even fifty years into the future in order to make responsible choices now, while we still have time.

Sometimes artists can see into the future better than policy makers can. H.G. Wells unleashed a terrifying vision of a possible future in his 1914 novel *The World Set Free*. Wells described a "nuclear" war long before anyone knew whether it would be possible to build a bomb: most of the world's capitals burning, consumed by a new kind of bomb, millions of people dead, all forms of government virtually at an end. Wells was prescient about the possible size of a bomb as well as about its destructive power. He wrote that the time would come when "a man could carry about in a handbag an amount of latent energy sufficient to wreck half a city." This in 1914! But it was only a novel.

From real life comes an exchange from a post-World War II Senate hearing that we might profitably listen to again:

Senator Byrd: What assurance has anybody got with

> a bomb that you can practically put
> in your pocket?

Dr. Langmuir: You cannot put them in your pocket.

Senator Johnson: You could put them in a suitcase.

Dr. Langmuir: I don't see any possibility of that.
If a gangster in his attic or cellar
can go out and make bombs and destroy anybody, I think the world is
about out.

--Special Committee on Atomic Energy, 1945

That atomic bombs might be easy to make and easy to hide sounds visionary, across the forty-year gulf that separates us from this hearing. If Senators could see that far into the abyss then, how did we end up here now, you might wonder.

Where we will end up forty years down the road might be a more profitable line of inquiry. Failure to come to grips with proliferation and to do battle against it is partly a function of our inability or unwillingness to see what kind of world it might create. National secur-ity war-gamers use "scenarios" to deal with this problem. How might nuclear war occur in a world where lots of countries and smaller groups have the bomb? There are any number of credible "nuclear war scenarios" for this kind of world, especially if you define "nuclear war" as one nuclear weapon exploded in anger (the only sensible definition ever set forth). Here are a few, but you could write your own as well, extrapolating from the daily news.

* In the late 1980s, Israel comes under great pres-sure to withdraw from the West Bank. A Palestinian demonstration gets out of hand and turns into a riot. The Israeli army puts it down ruthlessly, and several hundred Palestinians, including women and children, are killed. The next day Tel Aviv is destroyed by an atomic bomb for which no one claims responsibility.

* In the early 1990s, war breaks out again between

Iran and Iraq. Iran launches a massive chemical weapon attack in an effort to crush Iraq. The next day, the oil fields in southwestern Iran are destroyed by nuclear-armed cruise missiles. Iran retaliates by destroying Kirkuk with a bomb that was covertly planted in the city. Iran claims to have a second bomb secreted in Baghdad and threatens to detonate it unless Iraq surrenders at once.

* In the early 1990s, there is an uprising in the Indian state of Kashmir. The Indian army crushes the rebellion, killing thousands of rebels. Pakistan, which is covertly selling arms to Kashmir rebels and Sikhs in the Punjab, leads an international outcry. Conventionally armed Indian cruise missiles destroy all known Pakistani nuclear facilities. Pakistan loads its unacknowledged dozen nuclear bombs onto airplanes and launches an attack against Indian nuclear facilities. The Indians are prepared for the attack and destroy all of the Pakistani planes, although several penetrate Indian territory. One of the planes shot down in India carries two bombs with modern impact fuses and both bombs explode when the plane hits the ground. The rural area in which the bombs explode is immediately upwind of New Delhi, which is now threatened by massive fallout.

* All during the 1980s and early 1990s, East and West Germany continue their rapprochement, to the great discomfort of the Soviet Union and some European countries. Talk of reunification becomes an important political issue in the West. NATO is in disarray over new U.S. strategy formulations and control of nuclear weapons in Europe. The Federal Republic of Germany announces an independent nuclear weapons program, which has clearly been under way in secret for some years. The U.S. registers strong protests and threatens withdrawal of all U.S. forces. The Soviets respond immediately by attacking and destroying the two German weapons' facilities with low-yield nuclear weapons delivered by highly accurate cruise missiles. Simultaneously, the Soviets announce that they will under no conditions allow the reunification of Germany nor the arming of Germany with nuclear weapons, and that they are prepared to support that resolve by any and all means.

* Just after the turn of the century, Taiwan announces that it has covertly produced an arsenal of nuclear weapons, explodes a demonstration shot over the South China Sea, and demands membership in the United Nations. The Chinese government in Peking is outraged and calls on the United States and the Soviet Union to join it in demanding that Taiwan destroy all of its weapons and open its territory to multinational inspection. Peking further hints that if international means to halt the Taiwanese weapons program are not successful, it will use "all means necessary to eliminate this dire threat to the security and survival of China and the Chinese people."

******

By the definition of nuclear war we've introduced in this chapter--one nuclear weapon exploded in anger--we've already had a nuclear war, in August of 1945. There were, in fact, two nuclear weapons used against an enemy that had none, in a world that had no others. Would we have stopped at two if we had had any left? It's anybody's guess. The third bomb was already being assembled in the Pacific and would have been ready in a short time. It took Japan six days to surrender after Nagasaki. Good thing. We probably would have used the third bomb and others after it. And the idea that someone might use nuclear weapons as an instrument of terror might be far harder to erase from our minds.

In most of the nuclear war scenarios we've presented above, countries, not terrorists, are the actors. Even a cursory examination of the world suggests that those categories are not mutually exclusive: All it takes to blur the distinction is a crazed leader or cabal. The point we want to make in the following chapters is that if we can't prevent countries that might be reckless or desperate from getting the bomb, we probably can't stop smaller entities having even less to lose from getting it either. And if we can't stop them, will we be able to get through the next century without a nuclear war--even if it's "only" Washington or Moscow or Islamabad or Pretoria?

2

WHAT IT TAKES TO MAKE AN ATOMIC BOMB

How to Design an Atomic Bomb

> In some sort of crude sense
> which no vulgarity, no humor,
> no over-statement can quite
> extinguish, the physicists have
> known sin; and this is a know-
> ledge which they cannot lose.
> --J. Robert Oppenheimer

Unfortunately, it is also a knowledge which they cannot keep. The secret was inherent in $E = mc^2$ and once we forced that equation to yield an atomic bomb, it was only a matter of time before it wasn't a secret anymore. In fact, it was only four years until the Soviet Union was on to it.

It's been forty years now, and even kids are on to it. In 1970, a 14-year-old honors student held Orlando, Florida, hostage for a few hours with a ransom note and a credible atomic bomb blueprint. In 1977, a Princeton University physics major designed an atomic bomb that would cost $2,000 and weigh 125 pounds. It took four months. He didn't have to crack the secret himself: under the Freedom of Information Act, he ordered some $15 worth of government documents that pointed the way.

Designing a bomb is not the same as building it. The paperwork comes more easily to some minds than the nuts and bolts of engineering. But both kinds of skill are spread far and wide.

Knowing how to make the bomb is the end result of having eaten the apple (or of having opposable thumbs and a mind that works with them). That knowledge will last as long as the race does. However much the apple may stick in our throats when we see where it's brought us, there's no way back to the world we have lost.

The only way forward on the technological front is to control fissile material--the stuff of atomic bombs. For people who last studied physics back when atoms were like billiard balls, the next few pages may prove rough going. But billiard balls were a useful image in their time. Images may still be useful. You don't have to do the math to get the theory. But you have to get the theory to read the newspapers.

The basic design of an atomic bomb can be quite simple (see accompanying diagram). One way is to surround a core of enriched uranium or plutonium with conventional explosives. Dynamite will do in a pinch. Explode the dynamite, compressing the core into a smaller space, then quickly fire some neutrons at this compressed core from a neutron gun. You now have a "critical mass" and you have ignited a "chain reaction" in it.

The neutrons from the neutron gun split the first few uranium or plutonium atoms, or more precisely, split their nuclei. Particles start shooting off in all directions. Some of them are neutrons and they, in turn, split other nuclei and the explosion rapidly grows.

Building a bomb looks easy only in retrospect. Doing it the first time was quite another matter. Einstein's most famous equation became the common property of the world in 1905, but it took forty years to loose the power inherent in it. Einstein himself had said that splitting the atom seemed as unlikely as "shooting birds in the dark in a country where there are only a few birds." But during the thirties, the country looked less dark and the number of birds greater. At the Kaiser Wilhem Institute in Berlin, the Cavendish Laboratory in England, the Radium Institute in Paris, the Institute for Theoretical Physics in Copenhagen, at Columbia and Berkeley and Princeton in America, physicists were working at a frenetic pace to wrest from Einstein's theory the experimental breakthroughs it implied.

In 1938, French scientists were the first to devise an experiment that split the atom, but they didn't realize what they had done. Later that year, amid signs of imminent war in Europe, German scientists repeated the French experiment and drew the right conclusion from its puzzling results. They published their findings early in 1939, and set the world of physics aflame.

Most scientists thought the notion of going from splitting the atom to building an atomic bomb unlikely and, in the long tradition of science as an enterprise knowing no national boundaries, continued to publish

Atomic (Fission) Bomb

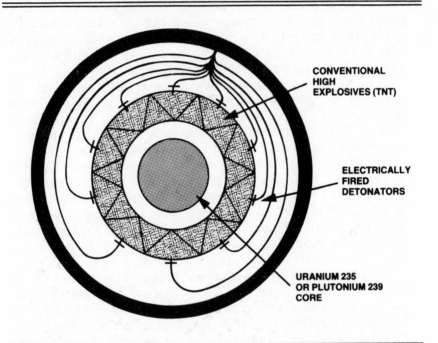

CONVENTIONAL
HIGH
EXPLOSIVES (TNT)

ELECTRICALLY
FIRED
DETONATORS

URANIUM 235
OR PLUTONIUM 239
CORE

Artwork, Michelle Higgins

papers on fission work all during 1939. It was proliferation of another sort--the spread of knowledge in a world already at war--and it went on in spite of the warning of European emigré scientists of the "remote but not negligible chance of grave misuse in Europe." It was not until June 1940 that American journal editors finally agreed to a voluntary blackout on fission papers.

Note: Besides knowledge and material, one must have a delivery system in order to pose a nuclear threat, but a caveat is in order here. While designing a delivery system that would work effectively over long distances has been a great challenge over the past generation, this is no longer so. Countries (or gangs) too poor in resources or knowledge to build bombs that fit in briefcases (as we and the Soviets can) might make do with much cruder counterparts that would fit into an oil drum or the trunk of a car. So the delivery system barrier has become much lower.

How to Get Bomb Material

There are two kinds of materials--plutonium and enriched uranium--that have been used as "bomb stuff" for first generation nuclear weapons. Both are becoming far too easy to obtain.

Plutonium. Named after the Greek god of the underworld, this silvery, unstable metal is a by-product produced when fuel in nuclear research reactors and nuclear power plants is burned. The world storehouse of this almost entirely man-made material is growing apace. The C.I.A. estimates that by the 1990s nuclear reactors "will be present on all continents, and at least 50 countries will have the capability to develop nuclear weapons."

Power plants mostly use uranium fuel, which is not in itself useful for weapons, usually in uranium-filled rods. The reactor produces heat by "burning" the uranium in its core. The real term for this "burning" is fissioning, and it means splitting the nuclei of the uranium atoms to produce heat and free neutrons. In commercial power plants, this heat is then transferred to a coolant, usually water, to make steam to run the turbines which make electricity. However, some of the free neutrons in the reactor core fuse with the nuclei of uranium atoms, turning them into plutonium--a suitable fissile material for use in nuclear explosives. To visualize this process better, picture the reactor core with its uranium rods as a squat cylinder big enough to fit in an ordinary elevator.

The reactor core is surrounded by a moderator, that is, some substance that will slow down and reflect some of the free neutrons, which would otherwise fly out into space, back into the core. The more free neutrons that don't escape, the more are available in the core to collide, causing fission or creating plutonium. The two most common moderators are two forms of water: light water, which is the same kind that comes out of the tap, and heavy water, in which the nucleus of the hydrogen atom contains not just a proton but also a neutron, which makes it more likely to reflect neutrons back into the core of the reactors. Reactors using light water must also use enriched uranium fuel in order to get a satisfactory number of atomic collisions. Heavy water, since it bounces more neutrons back into the core, allows a reactor to run on natural uranium.

If the point is producing bomb material, rather than electrical power or research, the reactor design is quite simple. It is also quite cheap: 99% of the cost of a power reactor lies in its cooling towers and complicated plumbing, and they can be dispensed with if you don't care about making electricity with the heat that is generated. All you need is the reactor core, the moderating blanket, some mechanisms for controlling and cooling the reactor, and two or three people to tend it. The technology was perfected by American physicists in the late forties, especially on the mesa at Los Alamos where a virtual cottage industry in small reactors developed with very limited capital and labor. A how-to manual for small reactors was published in the mid-fifties as part of the Atoms for Peace program.

The process of producing plutonium is fairly straightforward, once you have an operating reactor in which you can insert and withdraw additional fuel rods. You simply load a set of spare fuel rods with uranium oxide (not hard to obtain) and push them into the reactor and let them burn for a short time. The ideal is a quick toast, converting only about one percent of the uranium into plutonium. Cooking the rods longer will produce more of a wrong kind of plutonium, a heavier form that is not good for explosive use and could make a bomb fizzle instead of exploding. The heavier form of plutonium also makes the fuel rods even more radioactive.

The plutonium builds up inside the metal rods along with leftover uranium oxide and radioactive waste. To get at it you need a reprocessing plant. The rods are very hot--both in temperature and in radioactivity--so you need a hot cell, a room-sized, lead-lined container equipped with remote control arms. The robot arms push the fuel rods into a guillotine that chops them into small pieces. The pieces drop into a nitric acid bath and dissolve. A solvent is then added to precipitate the plutonium in metallic form--the stuff of bombs. This process is easy and cheap enough for every country except China to have used it for its first bomb test.

There are ostensibly peaceable uses for plutonium. During the 1970s, when we thought the world might in a few decades run out of uranium that is easy to find and mine, plutonium looked like a good alternate power source. But a good many new sources of natural uranium have been discovered, nuclear power has not grown as fast as predicted, and for now the world has more uranium than it needs.

Back when uranium looked like a scarce commodity, we invented the breeder reactor, which uses plutonium as the fuel in the reactor core. The plutonium is surrounded by a blanket of uranium. As the reactor operates, more plutonium is created in the blanket and in the core than is used up in the core, thus breeding new fuel. Here's how the Atomic Energy Commission described the process in a promo poster: "Johnny had three truckloads of plutonium. He used three of them to light New York for one year. How much plutonium did Johnny have left? Answer: four truckloads." What the AEC didn't ask, for obvious reasons, is how many pounds of plutonium it takes to make an atomic bomb. Answer: about fifteen. How many bombs could Johnny make from his four truckloads if he decided he didn't want New York to light up at all next year?

Backing off on development of the breeder reactor would be hard to do, even if the world community recognized that plutonium is the likeliest route to a terrorist bomb. France, Britain, West Germany, Japan, and the

Soviet Union have committed substantial support to research and development. The United States, which is quite rich in uranium deposits, has backed off on breeder reactor development. Particularly for West Germany, France, Britain, and Japan, however, limited native uranium deposits make breeder reactors look like a promising way to conserve their stores: Breeders use uranium fifty to one-hundred times more efficiently than other reactors do. Unfortunately, they could also breed bombs quite efficiently: Breeder reactor fuel pellets are so rich in plutonium that they can be turned directly into bombs.

Enriched uranium. To make a bomb with uranium, you have to isolate the kind of uranium (the isotope Uranium 235 or U^{235}) that will carry on a chain reaction. The uranium existing in nature is 99% the wrong kind (the isotope Uranium 238--U^{238}) for making bombs. The most widely used way to enrich uranium to a bomb-grade percentage of U^{235} is gaseous diffusion. The second most popular method is centrifuging. A third process using high-powered lasers is being developed, and a fourth, an aerodynamic process called the Becker nozzle, is used in South Africa, West Germany, and perhaps Israel and Argentina.

In a gaseous diffusion plant, like our huge facility at Oak Ridge, Tennessee, uranium hexafluoride is forced through a semi-permeable membrane in one tank after another. Since U^{235} is slightly lighter than U^{238}, it passes through the membrane slightly faster. The key word here is *slightly*. It takes about four thousand membrane passes to get the end product up to 93%--the right kind of uranium to make bombs. The plant at Oak Ridge consists of about sixty acres of rooms full of tanks connected by plumbing pipes. It is very quiet, with a low hum coming from all directions at once. There are only a few workers, mostly technicians who make rounds from time to time to be sure there are no gas leaks. It takes months to get all the stages synchronized and running efficiently in a plant of this character. And it takes a lot of power--which was one reason for building the plant in Tennessee Valley Authority country. In fact, during the 1950s, the plant was consuming 15% of all the electricity produced in the United

States.

The second technique for obtaining U^{235}, the high speed gaseous centrifuge, is technically more advanced. We also have a centrifuge test plant at Oak Ridge and a larger facility being built near Portsmouth, Ohio. Like gaseous diffusion, centrifuge separation uses uranium hexafluoride gas, and is made possible by the fact that U^{235} is slightly lighter than U^{238}.

Gas centrifuges are in principle much like the spinning devices which some people use in their kitchens to remove the water from just-washed lettuce leaves. Just as spinning those gadgets forces the water to the walls of the canister, spinning a gaseous centrifuge forces the gas with a high concentration of heavier U^{238} atoms to the walls while that with more of the lighter U^{235} atoms collects in the middle.

Centrifuges have been used for a long time in medical research. However, this approach only became feasible for producing bomb material in the 1960s when the ultra-high-speed centrifuge was perfected; earlier models didn't spin fast enough for this purpose. The centrifuges used at the Oak Ridge plant are bigger than those used in medical research (the size of very tall oil drums versus elongated oatmeal canisters), but otherwise much the same. A full-sized centrifuge plant for commercial production of U^{235} might cover about twenty acres and would be a good deal more energy efficient per pound of bomb material produced than is the gaseous diffusion plant. Unlike the perhaps four thousand stages required to create bomb stuff in gaseous diffusion, centrifuge enrichment requires perhaps thirty-five stages. And much smaller plants--like one for a covert bomb-stuff factory--are, of course, possible, although both centrifuge enrichment plants and gaseous diffusion plants are usually quite large.

One disadvantage of this technique is that when the centrifuge breaks, it doesn't just quietly leak like the gaseous diffusion plant tanks. It creates mayhem. In 1973, a rotor broke in one of the Oak Ridge centrifuges. The centrifuges have heavy walls to contain the shrapnel that a broken rotor becomes at such high speeds. But the broken pieces hit those walls whirling so fast that they set the outside walls to whirling and broke the centrifuge loose from all its pipes. It lurched about the room setting all the other centrifuges free from their moorings as well, a sort of grotesque atomic dance.

A third uranium enrichment process that is even more energy efficient than centrifuges is laser separation. The Lawrence Livermore Laboratories in California have developed a laboratory-scale version of this process, and the Department of Energy has plans to build a laser separation plant near Portsmouth, Ohio, at a cost of $3 billion.

The laser was invented in 1960, initially using a rod of ruby crystal. However, by the *late 1960s* it was clear that many other things would "lase." The laser is essentially a sharply focused column of light that can do lots of things, including kicking atoms into a more excited state than normal. It was recognized early on that laser separation of U^{235} was potentially feasible, if a laser could be found at the right wavelength and with enough power. The mid-seventies saw the development of the tunable laser, that is, a laser capable of being tuned to any frequency of light. The first tunable lasers were very low-powered, and it was a real challenge to invent a high-powered one at the right wavelength for uranium.

Another problem was finding the right form of uranium to process. Uranium hexafluoride, which becomes a gas at 57 degrees C and works fine for gaseous diffusion, doesn't work very well for laser separation. Finally it was found that vaporized metallic uranium works, but it only becomes a gas at several thousand degrees C and is highly corrosive as well.

The laser separation process which has emerged as potentially feasible requires two laser "kicks." The first kick comes from a laser finely tuned in the infrared part of the spectrum (shorter than visible light) to take advantage of the fine distinctions between U^{235} and U^{238}. The challenge is to excite only the U^{235} atoms. In the process developed, the laser light shines into a very thin uranium vapor. In order to use all the laser light efficiently, i.e., absorb all of the light so as not to waste it, the chamber of uranium vapor must be hundreds of meters long. But if using up lots of power is no problem, shorter chambers could be used.

When the production chamber is full of a large number of excited U^{235} atoms, a second laser in the ultraviolet spectrum, longer than visible light, is aimed at it, making the U^{235} atoms ionize (lose an electron and become positively charged). The ionized U^{235} atoms are then collected with a magnetic field.

The laser method of separating out U^{235} is attractive because it does the job 30% more efficiently than centrifuging (which is itself ten times as efficient as gaseous diffusion). But we have spent a billion dollars on fifteen years of research and we still don't have a production-sized plant. The Soviet Union is working on this new technology, as are France, Israel, and Brazil.

Enriched uranium is also used as a fuel in nuclear power plants or research reactors. The power plants in the United States and most other countries use low enriched uranium fuel--a form that is only 3% the right stuff (U^{235}). However, many research reactors all over the world use a more potent form that is fully weapons-grade, that is, above 90% enriched uranium. As with plutonium, the same fuel can produce power or research or, with some added steps, bombs. "What do you want it for?" is the obvious question to ask countries that ask to buy fissionable material or the technology that might produce it. But how can you tell if you're getting a straight answer?

So what does all this mean in terms of who gets the bomb? The simple fact is that the technical barriers to obtaining bomb material are melting away like a snowball in the Sahara. Within the next few decades, the technologies described here will become more widely available. For now, producing plutonium in crude reactors and separating it by spent fuel reprocessing looks like the best route for a country (or a group smaller than that) short on scientists and engineers. The uranium enrichment techniques currently require more sophistication and access to a substantial amount of electrical power.

But this only means that it will be easier for nation-states than for terrorist groups to exploit these emerging technologies. At least for now. But, in time, even these new technologies will become off-the-shelf items. We simply must recognize this fact: we are irreversibly entering an era in which a committed group smaller than a nation-state can covertly produce bombs in a facility no bigger than a grade school or a small warehouse.

This is indeed a problem for those of us who will

live and act over the next thirty or forty years. But to attack this problem effectively, we have to understand the *past* thirty or forty years and see the process of proliferation whole. In the next four chapters we will try to do that, and in Chapter 7 we will present options that could help us find our way out of the labyrinth.

3

BARRIERS TO BUILDING THE BOMB
AND WHERE THEY FAILED

Where you date the beginning of the nuclear prolifer-ation problem depends on your point of view. For some physicists, it began when work continued on the Manhattan Project even after Nazi Germany had surrendered. For most Americans, it began when the Soviets exploded their first bomb in 1949. For much of the world, especially the Russians, the British, the French, and the Chinese, it became a real problem when their neighbors got the bomb or more efficient means of delivering it. However, no matter how you cut it, from one country with nuclear weapons in 1945 to seven or eight or nine in 1985, this is hardly a success story.

The history of nuclear non-proliferation efforts is a sorry succession of barriers erected, barriers failing, and new barriers established, only to fail themselves. If we are to do any better in the future, we must first understand why we have failed in the past. So let's take a look at what we have tried, with an eye toward under-standing that failure.

One Nuclear Power: 1945-1949

If the question "How many nuclear-weapons states should there be in the world?" had been posed in the early 1940s, we would have answered "If Germany has it, two." As it turned out, Germany didn't have it, and there was only one nuclear power in 1945.

When it became clear in the immediate aftermath of World War II that the Soviet Union aspired to world-power status and deemed military might the best means to that end, we continued to manufacture and stockpile atomic bombs.

Enough Already! At the same time, however, Washington recognized that a world in which many nations had nuclear weapons would be extremely dangerous. So it began a campaign to keep the technology from spreading. The first U.S. initiative was the Baruch Plan, a proposal to the United Nations to establish an international agency that would take control of all nuclear facilities and materials worldwide. Once that mechanism was in place, assuring that no other country could make nuclear weapons, the United States would destroy all its own.

The Soviet Union, not trusting America's intent, countered with a plan under which the U.S. would destroy its atomic bombs *before* an international system preventing other countries from making them was established. The United States, equally mistrustful, found the Soviet proposal unacceptable.

Here was the world's first attempt at nuclear arms control and it couldn't work because Americans and Russians couldn't trust each other. Sound familiar? In fact, I.I Rabi, a physicist who worked on the Baruch Plan, said recently on television that Baruch himself didn't believe the plan was serious. Rabi also raised the question of whether the United States put much effort into promoting it or making it palatable to the Russians.

At this juncture, the United States launched a unilateral effort to hold onto its status as the world's only nuclear-weapons state. An act of Congress passed in 1946 outlawed disclosure of any information about nuclear weapons--even to its World War II allies like Britain, France, and Canada. The United States also intensified its futile effort to gain control of all known uranium deposits in the world.

Oops! In 1949, the Soviet Union exploded its first atomic bomb, made from the ore of Siberian uranium deposits. Soviet physicists, with some outside help, had simply plugged away at the technology until they'd worked it out.

So much for secrecy and uranium monopolies. There wasn't much the United States could do against a technically advanced nation with ready access to uranium.

Two Nuclear Powers: 1949-1952

Enough Already! When its most likely adversary got the bomb, the U.S. began looking at other countries as potential nuclear powers as well. Countries like Israel, India, and Argentina were beginning to explore the possibilities of atomic energy, but they were all fairly undeveloped, long on domestic problems and short on scientific and economic resources.

The advanced nations of Western Europe--those with the most potential for going nuclear--were America's friends and America thought it could stop them. The U.S. entered into the North Atlantic Treaty and provided them with strong security guarantees: An attack against one is an attack against all. Not long after, when it became clear that the Soviets would keep their large standing armies in Eastern Europe and the Western alliance was unwilling to match them, the U.S. added a nuclear component to its commitment. The U.S. hoped that that promise, along with closing the door on nuclear weapons collaboration and Europe's need to recover from the devastation of World War II, would keep its European partners off the nuclear track.

Oops! In October 1952, Britain conducted its first nuclear-weapons test. It wasn't just that it didn't trust America to keep its promises, though that was one argument for building a British bomb. Another impetus for the decision to go for the bomb was that Britain had shared a good many of its secrets and much of its talent with America during World War II and didn't like being treated like a second-class power just because it was losing its empire.

So much for security guarantees. Even an ironclad alliance with the greatest nuclear power extant could look like a less than reliable guarantee.

Three Nuclear Powers: 1952-1960

Enough Already! Monopolies on uranium and technology were out of the question and security guarantees didn't seem to be a sufficient barrier. So the United States changed the focus of its non-proliferation policy. Many nations of the world had gotten excited about the potential of atomic energy for peaceful uses, particularly generating electricity. The U.S. proposed that instead of trying to deny nuclear technology to other nations, it would actually provide the requisite know-how, equipment, and materials for nuclear power plants *as long as all the recipients promised not to try to make nuclear weapons.* The new policy was announced by President Eisenhower in a speech before the United Nations General Assembly on December 8, 1953.

The no-nukes pledge entailed in this "Atoms for Peace" program would be enforced through periodic inspections of all nuclear facilities in recipient countries. Although the United States would conduct these inspections to begin with, eventually that function would be taken over by an international organization--the International Atomic Energy Agency, established in Vienna in 1957.

Atoms for Peace was a hit, and the United States ultimately entered into cooperative agreements with thirty nations during the fifties and sixties. During the same period, Britain, France, Canada, and West Germany also launched nuclear export programs, although not all their early agreements contained the inspection restrictions mandated by the United States.

Oops! Citing the vulnerability of the United States to new, longer-range Soviet missiles and a presumed consequent weakening of the U.S. commitment to protect Western Europe, France exploded its first nuclear test in February of 1960.

So much for buying a global commitment to non-proliferation. Guaranteeing Atoms for Peace did nothing to guarantee security for countries in the shadow of existing nuclear powers.

Four Nuclear Powers: 1960-1964

Enough Already! Even as the United States was discovering--by a process of elimination--that unilateral approaches to stopping nuclear proliferation were ineffective, the rest of the world's non-nuclear nations (or most of them) were recognizing the potential utility of cooperative efforts.

The most promising of these cooperative efforts was the International Atomic Energy Agency, which developed a broad "safeguards" program in the early 1960s. In addition to taking over the on-site facilities inspection tasks from the nuclear exporters, or supplier nations, IAEA's multinational staff audited and counterchecked the records of nuclear materials entering a facility and what was done with them. It monitored facility operations with cameras and placed seals in various places in these facilities to prevent fissionable material from being diverted between scheduled inventories. The IAEA's role was made more complex by the fact that it was also intended to facilitate the sharing of nuclear technology and was thus both watchdog and promoter, not an easy act to balance.

Limitations on the effectiveness of IAEA operations were--and are--self-evident. It could only inspect facilities that nations agreed to place under safeguards, that is, those using equipment or materials supplied by nations which made IAEA monitoring part of the condition of sale, or indigenously produced plants that countries volunteered to put under Agency coverage. Some suppliers required no IAEA safeguards, especially during the 1950s. In any case, nuclear facilities that nations developed on their own--India, Pakistan, Argentina, and Brazil have done so--were all too frequently not placed under inspection.

Moreover, there have been ongoing problems with the implementation of the safeguards themselves. Nations have the right to reject inspectors from whatever countries they choose. As a consequence, for instance, Iraqi facilities were only inspected by Soviet and Hungarian nationals between 1976 and 1981. Inspections are usually announced three months in advance, giving determined cheaters time to try to cover up their misdeeds. The seals used by the agency are not absolutely tamper-proof. Film and video monitoring are subject to a variety of problems: Images are sometimes unclear, objects or people may block the camera's view, and sometimes the cameras simply don't work for days or weeks at a time.

Another approach to inhibiting nuclear proliferation is to halt all testing of nuclear devices--a so-called comprehensive test ban. Although testing is not essential for reliable, if crude, atomic bombs, it is necessary for "advanced" projects such as building hydrogen bombs and compact warheads for missiles. The world community pursued this approach, but without the support of key nations such as France and China. Verification problems and fluctuations in East-West relations made progress slow, however, and what emerged in 1963 after eight years of on-again, off-again negotiation was a partial test ban treaty. The treaty in reality responded only to growing alarm about the effects of drifting radioactive fallout from atmospheric tests: It prohibited tests of nuclear weapons in the atmosphere, in outer space, and underwater. The Limited Test Ban Treaty did little, however, to contribute to non-proliferation efforts. It failed to ban underground tests, and, most importantly, it failed to get all the then-nuclear powers as signatories: France, the fourth nuclear weapons state at the time, refused to sign. So did China.

Oops! In 1964, the People's Republic of China exploded its first nuclear device--above ground, like all other nations' first shots. Since China hadn't signed the Limited Test Ban Treaty it was under no obligation to abide by it. And because it developed the facilities that produced its weapons on its own, or claimed to have done so, IAEA safeguards were irrelevant.

So much for test bans and safeguards. They could only be completely effective if they were universally accepted.

Five Nuclear Powers: 1964-1974

Enough Already! Initiatives toward a global non-proliferation agreement had been introduced in the UN General Assembly since 1961. China's getting the bomb in 1964 suddenly made them look more crucial.

Although the NATO nuclear weapons states, the Soviet Union, and the non-nuclear states of Western Europe brought conflicting interests to the bargaining table, a satisfactory nuclear non-proliferation agreement was ready to be signed by mid-1968.

The Treaty on the Non-Proliferation of Nuclear Weapons (commonly called the Non-Proliferation Treaty-- the NPT) went into effect on March 1, 1970, and had the following provisions:

1. No nuclear weapons states would provide nuclear weapons to non-nuclear weapons states;

2. All the peaceful nuclear activities--not just those with inspections mandated by the seller or offered up by a country that built them itself--of non-nuclear weapons states would be put under safeguards to ensure

that they would not be diverted to the manufacture of nuclear weapons. (Some of the nuclear weapons states later 'offered' to put some of their own civilian facilities under the safeguards, though the Soviet Union signed a formal agreement to this effect with the IAEA only in early 1985 and China has yet to do so.)

3. Peaceful uses of nuclear energy would be made available to non-nuclear weapons states under appropriate international supervision, that is, IAEA safeguards; and

4. Nuclear-weapons states would "pursue negotiations in good faith on effective measures relating to cessation of the nuclear arms race at an early date and to nuclear disarmament, and on a treaty on general and complete disarmament under strict and effective international controls."

Another provision of the treaty was that its operation would be reviewed by the signatories at five-year intervals.

By the end of 1973, 81 of the nations in the U.N. had signed and ratified the treaty. Unfortunately, in spite of substantial persuasive efforts launched by the United States, the Soviet Union, and other treaty architects, a number of key countries had failed to sign. These included nuclear states such as France and China, and important potential nuclear states such as India, Israel, South Africa, Pakistan, Brazil, and Argentina. In addition, because of the behavior of some signatories, including intemperate statements by their leaders, the signatures of several nations, such as Iraq and Libya, were increasingly suspect. There has been some progress over the past decade: By early 1985, 123 of the 159 nations in the U.N. had signed.

Oops! In May 1974, India stunned the world by conducting what it called a "peaceful nuclear explosion." India had bought the reactor that produced nuclear material for the device from Canada in 1955, with no safeguards imposed on it as part of the sale. The fissile material for the explosion came from a reprocessing plant India built on its own. Why weren't these facilities subject to safeguards? Simple: India didn't sign the non-proliferation treaty and had never made a political commitment not to develop nuclear explosives.

It is also widely believed that Israel--another country that has refused to sign the NPT--began to manufacture the various components for nuclear weapons in the late 1960s or early 1970s, using an unsafeguarded French reactor bought in 1958 and an Israeli-built reprocessing plant.

So much for non-proliferation by treaty. It's good as far as it goes, but it's hardly good enough unless everyone can be persuaded to sign.

Six, Seven, Eight, Nine Nuclear Powers: 1974-19??

Enough Already! The Indian nuclear explosion and the growing evidence of an Israeli bomb demonstrated the frailty of the world non-proliferation regime, NPT, IAEA, and all. The countries that sell nuclear technology and materials then got together to see how they could use their collective power more effectively to stem the proliferation tide.

Soon after the Indian test, representatives from the United States, Canada, Australia, Britain, France, Belgium, West Germany, Italy, Japan, the Netherlands, Sweden, Switzerland, the Soviet Union, Czechoslovakia, East Germany, and Poland got together in London to discuss ways to control the export of sensitive technologies. This, in time, led to what was known as the London Suppliers Group. This group and others helped develop a "trigger list" of exports that would require the application of IAEA safeguards. Over the following three years, until its dissolution in 1977, the Suppliers Group tightened its guidelines banning the export of specific nuclear equipment except for that under safeguards and agreements prohibiting its use for nuclear explosions of any kind--however "peaceful" they might be made to seem.

Some major nuclear suppliers such as the United States have been promoting nuclear export policies that the Group as a whole will not adopt. Chief among these is requiring application of IAEA safeguards on all nuclear activities--so-called full-scope safeguards--in a recipient state as a condition of sale. Since 1976, Canada, Australia, and the United States have adopted this policy independently and the Soviet Union is generally adhering to it as well. Such supplier nations as France, West Germany, and Switzerland continue to require application of IAEA safeguards only on the facility (usually a nuclear power plant) involved in a particular sale, rather than on *all* facilities in the recipient state.

The importance of avoiding full-scope safeguards if a country is intent on developing nuclear weapons is illustrated by a recent sale to Argentina. In spite of its crushing international debt, Argentina agreed to pay West Germany and Switzerland *a half billion dollars more* for a reactor complex than Canada would have charged for the same facilities. Reason: Canada would have made the sale contingent on application of full-scope IAEA safeguards in Argentina.

In addition to discussion concerning sales of nuclear power plants, the Suppliers Group/Zangger Committee discussions have also focused on the export of "sensitive nuclear technologies"--technology and equipment for reprocessing plutonium from spent nuclear power-plant fuel rods, as well as equipment used to enrich uranium. India's nuclear explosion using plutonium from reprocessed spent nuclear fuel proved that the "civilian" applications of sensitive technology nuclear fuels could not be definitively separated from its military applications. Controlling the export of this technology thus seems essential to obstructing the development of nuclear weapons.

Even assuming that the major nuclear suppliers could agree on a set of more effective export rules, they still will not be able to prevent determined governments from eventually developing nuclear weapons on their own. Indeed, they have not yet persuaded France, Germany, or Switzerland to agree that *all* of a country's nuclear facilities should come under IAEA safeguards, not just the piece of equipment on the bill of sale. The Suppliers Group has agreed informally to "exercise restraint" in transfering sensitive technologies, and France and West Germany have declared that they won't export such technologies either.

In the summer of 1984, members of the Suppliers Group (except the Eastern Bloc countries) met secretly in Luxembourg to discuss supplier issues, including, specifically, a proposal that all Western suppliers require application of full-scope safeguards in recipient countries as a condition of major nuclear supply. All twelve countries supported the plan's goal--a halt to proliferation--but only Canada, Australia, and Britain spoke for the specific U.S. initiative. "Well, we'll do it if everybody else does" was a common dodge. Worries cropped up on three main fronts: losing export revenue, driving less developed countries toward "nuclear independence," and losing a share of the market to emerging nuclear suppliers such as countries like Argentina and China that are now able to compete for nuclear trade.

The Luxembourg meeting broke up without reaching consensus on specific policies. Even more dismaying is what happened afterward. U.S. officials reportedly leaked the story to a newspaper, thus raising the ire of France and several other countries that said they had only agreed to come to the meeting on the condition that it be kept secret. As one observer commented: "It was no small accomplishment just to get some of these people to sit down together in the same room. Whether we'll be able to do that again, as a result of the leaks, is a question that remains to be seen."

Even if major nuclear suppliers can somehow be brought together again--and manage to reach agreement on more stringent conditions of sale--there's a whole new set of potential nuclear supplier nations emerging, including China, Argentina, India, and Brazil. They want the international prestige and the foreign revenues that accrue from nuclear technology sales. How are they to be persuaded that preventing nuclear proliferation is more important than the obvious benefits of trade?

At present, the international non-proliferation system consists of the following elements:

1. The Nuclear Non-Proliferation Treaty. A commitment by non-nuclear-weapons state signatories not to seek to acquire nuclear explosive devices and a commitment by nuclear-weapons states not to assist them to do so. Not yet a completely effective set of rules of international conduct--and never likely to be one as long as critical countries such as China, France, and India reject it and as long as the nuclear-weapons states party to the treaty, particularly the United States and the Soviet

Union, fail to reach agreement on limiting and reducing their own nuclear arsenals.

2. The International Atomic Energy Agency. Monitors nuclear facilities using techniques and rules that might miss the determined cheater who is willing to take a chance. Functions without enforcement or sanction powers, except the sanction of exposure to the world community.

3. The Nuclear Supplier Group. A group of supplier nations that agreed during the mid-1970s to require application of IAEA safeguards as a condition of sale for certain kinds of nuclear exports. Doesn't yet include the new supplier nations and cannot even get the old ones to agree on the most stringent export rules. Not yet clear whether consensus on ironclad rules is possible.

4. The Zangger Committee. A group of 21 nuclear supplier nations chaired by a Swiss official who is also a physicist. These nations have agreed on a trigger list of material and equipment the export of which should trigger application of safeguards on the recipient facility as a condition of supply. The list is focused narrowly on technology useful to weapons programs, but only recently (at the State Department's request) was the list broadened to include ultracentrifuges.

5. Security Guarantees. A commitment to defend certain states in the event of hostile attack by another, often used as an inducement to potential proliferators to forego the nuclear option. Many West European and Asian countries have not pursued nuclear explosive development programs because they have received such guarantees from the United States. However, it is not yet clear in all cases the extent to which confidence in such guarantees will continue.

Oops, Oops, Oops? The history of international efforts to build a wall against nuclear proliferation has been one of adding bricks to the wall too late to prevent more countries slipping over it, around it, or under it. There can be little confidence that the wall constructed of the bricks described above will withstand the next assault. The question is not whether current barriers will be breached, but when and by what countries.

Can a determined human effort build the wall high enough so that, in time, it holds and halts the growth in nuclear-weapons states--the second nuclear arms race--at some manageable level? In order that there might be hope of halting the third nuclear arms race--nuclear terrorism--before it begins? In order that our descendants may look back at us and see our fears as having been as ill-founded as those of 1960--when there was fear that there would be twenty or more countries with the bomb by today?

Can the imperfectly made and imperfectly laid bricks in today's wall be refurbished and reset in a more effective edifice--and built higher and stronger with new bricks, so that someday the barrier holds?

We will take up this challenge in Chapter 7, but first we will take a much closer look at just how the various nuclear powers and would-be nuclear powers have so far managed to breach the wall.

4

THE NUCLEAR CLUB:
UNITED STATES, SOVIET UNION,
BRITAIN, FRANCE, AND CHINA

A country that has nuclear material and know-how needs only one more thing to build the bomb: the will to do so. The motives underlying that will are mainly security and prestige. The obvious first answer to "Why build the bomb?" is security. Every country that has built the bomb decided to do so in order to try to protect itself in a dangerous world. Prestige also figures in most countries' choices, but is a decidedly secondary motive, far down the scale compared to security. The very fact that the Nuclear Club is becoming less exclusive all the time erodes prestige as a motive. Joining the club is not the certain route to national pride that it once was.

United States, 1945

Why Build the Bomb?

Imagine how World War II would have ended if Germany had been able to fit its V-2 rockets with atomic bombs. The war in Europe would have been over in a day, and likely the rest of the war as well. America's desperate need to be the first to build the bomb was a given since the survival of all the Allied countries depended on getting it before Germany did. As it happened, Germany had already surrendered when the U.S. detonated the first test bomb, Trinity, on July 16, 1945. Japan had a fledgling atomic bomb project at the beginning of the war, but it made little progress.

Since the United States is the only country to have used atomic bombs in an act of war, a second question is in order: Why use the bomb? Motives for using the bomb on Japanese cities are murkier than those for building it. The only official voice against using the bomb was that of General Dwight Eisenhower, who in July of 1945 expressed "grave misgivings" to Secretary of War Henry

Stimson. Japan was already beaten in Eisenhower's view, and world opinion would damn the United States for using such a terrible weapon. Leo Szilard, a Hungarian refugee physicist, organized opposition among fellow scientists who worked on the Manhattan Project. In a report to Stimson in June 1945, a group of them argued against using the bomb and warned that a nuclear arms race was inevitable since other countries would soon produce atomic bombs. Szilard also got 69 colleagues to sign a petition to President Truman arguing for a demonstration shot on a desert island, on the theory that no enemy that knew what an atomic bomb could do would continue fighting.

As it happened, Japan did not surrender immediately after Hiroshima. Three days later the U.S. dropped another bomb on Nagasaki. One could argue that Hiroshima was to end the war without the estimated one million American casualties that an invasion of Japan would exact and that Nagasaki was revenge--for Pearl Harbor, for the Japanese death camps, for the kamikaze attacks, for the savagery of the island-to-island last stand in the final days of the war. But the historical record suggests that neither bomb was seen in such a manner. Atomic bombs were simply viewed as a far easier and less costly method for systematically destroying Japan's cities, a process that had already begun with massive B-29 raids on Tokyo and elsewhere. U.S. military planners thought that defeating Japan might require using a large number of atomic bombs and were operating on a virtual "fire when ready" standing order. President Truman was en route to America from the Potsdam Conference when the bomb was dropped on Nagasaki, and the standing order meant there was no need to consult him.

To understand the decision to use atomic bombs, one must have a real sense of what World War II was like for Americans. Many families had lost a husband or a son, and even though America entered the war more than two years after it began, it had been a long war, nearly four years. The reaction of a good many Americans to the use of the atomic bomb against Japan is reflected in the comment of one soldier who had fought in the European theater and had been taken prisoner by the Nazis. After some months as a prisoner of war, he was liberated by fellow soldiers when the Third Reich fell. He got 60 days' leave in America, and was scheduled to be shipped out for the final assault on Japan, when, in his words, "Harry dropped that beautiful bomb."

Prestige was not a prime motive in America's initial decision to build the bomb. It probably did figure later in its decision not to share its discoveries with its allies. As early as 1943, relations between American and British scientists doing fission work were soured by mutual suspicion. The United States did not want to give Britain secrets that might figure in postwar industrial competition. It also feared that secrets shared with Britain might leak to Germany or the Soviet Union.

Who Helped?

In the thirties, British scientists were closer to cracking the secret of the atomic bomb than Americans were. In fact, it was the British who told the United States that the bomb was possible. By 1940, the best British scientists had to turn their attention to developing air defenses to combat the Luftwaffe, particularly radar, and most fission work was abandoned. However, British scientists did share what they knew with their American counterparts. There were also French scientists at work on the Manhattan Project. Isidor Rabi, a Russian-born physicist working on radar at MIT, consulted on the project. But the real outside help on the first atomic bomb came from physicists who had fled Hitler's Europe: Enrico Fermi from Italy, Leo Szilard and Edward Teller from Hungary, Niels Bohr from Denmark, and Otto Frisch and Rudolph Peierls from Austria.

Notes

When President Truman told Stalin at Potsdam about the atomic bomb his advisers watched Stalin's reaction to see if he would blanch. Whatever his reaction at the time, he was able to say blandly later, "I do not consider the atomic bomb as such a serious force. Atomic bombs are intended to frighten people with weak nerves." Truman did not believe the Manhattan Project scientists' warning about an eventual nuclear arms race, probably because his advisers had incorrectly told him that the Soviet Union lacked significant uranium deposits. In

1946 he had the following conversation with J. Robert Oppenheimer:

Truman: When will the Russians be able to build the bomb?

Oppenheimer: I don't know.

Truman: I know.

Oppenheimer: When?

Truman: Never.

Soviet Union, 1949

Why Build the Bomb?

"Never" turned out to be three more years. Stalin's scoffing remark about weak nerves didn't cut any ice with Soviet physicists. After the first Soviet test, physicist Vassily Emelyanov asked, "What would have happened if we hadn't made it? They would have shot us. Just shot."

Here we see an early version of the doctrine of deterrence: The Soviets got the bomb to deter the United States from using it. As the Soviet arsenal grew to the point where it posed a serious threat to the United States, deterrence became the main justification for building up the American arsenal as well.

Prestige was a distant second motivation far behind security, but nonetheless part of the Soviet decision to build the bomb.

Who Helped?

The Soviets got help from physicist Klaus Fuchs, who had been a youth leader of the Communist Party in his hometown in Germany before Hitler came to power. He worked on the bomb at Los Alamos and later was part of the American team that developed the conceptual framework for the H-bomb. He had been passing atomic secrets to the Soviets for years when he was finally arrested in London in 1950. "I had complete confidence in Russian policy," he admitted, "and I believed that the Western Allies deliberately allowed Russia and Germany to fight each other to the death. I therefore had no hesitation in giving all the information I had." One of his contacts was the brother-in-law of Julius Rosenberg (who, along with his wife Ethel, was executed as a spy in 1951).

The motive for treasonous acts by a handful of people with access to classified information on the bomb is easier to understand when put in the context of the times. The Stalin purges were unknown in the West, and communism exerted a powerful appeal for many intellectuals during the thirties and forties, before it was discredited by the reports of Stalin's butchery. Even Oppenheimer, who was profoundly loyal to his country, came to grief in 1954 because of his relations in the early forties with family members and friends who had communist leanings.

The Soviets could have made the bomb without help, but it would have taken them longer. Soviet scientists had begun exploring the possibilities of fission in 1939, but physicist Igor Kurchatov was not called to Moscow and assigned to work on an atomic bomb until the summer of 1942. Many Soviet scientists were in the army or assigned to more immediately pressing war work. Some of the best laboratories were damaged or destroyed in the fight to repel Hitler's invading forces. By spring 1943, Kurchatov had assembled twenty colleagues and begun work, but there were many conflicting ideas about how to proceed and they didn't have a single ounce of pure uranium. Stalin was alarmed at the progress Oppenheimer was making at Los Alamos and pushed the group to catch up with America. Truman's Potsdam revelation about the Los Alamos bomb thus came as no surprise, though the Americans couldn't have known that at the time. The nuclear reactor near Moscow finally reached critical mass on Christmas Day in 1946. The first Soviet bomb was detonated on August 29, 1949, in the deserts of Kazakhstan.

Britain, 1952

Why Build the Bomb?

The U.S. said, "Trust us, our bombs will keep anybody from attacking you," but the British were skeptical. World War II was a fresh memory, as was the isolationism of America in the period between the wars. Britain had faced the German onslaught on the Western front alone until Pearl Harbor brought America into the war, and might again have to stand alone against enormous odds. The bomb thus seemed a prudent and relatively cheap hedge against an American withdrawal from Europe. Uncertainties about the character of the American alliance were probably confirmed when Congress closed the door on nuclear collaboration with America's wartime allies in the 1946 Atomic Energy Act. By 1947, Britain had begun its own pursuit of the bomb.

Clement Attlee, British Prime Minister at the time of his nation's first atomic test, laid out the prestige question for all the world to see: "The Americans were rather apt to think they were the big boys and we were the small boys; we'd just got to show them that they didn't know everything." By the late forties, the sun had begun to set on the British Empire, which was in economic decline and was losing its overseas colonies. Getting the bomb guaranteed Britain's place as a first-rate second-class power, ensured that it would still have a voice in world affairs and some leverage with its powerful American ally. The success of the latter aim is clear. The "special relationship" between America and Britain recognized in the 1958 Bilateral Agreement for Nuclear Sharing continues to the present day.

Who Helped?

To British scientists, the first bomb was as British as it was American. Some of Britain's finest were there at the conception. They didn't need outside help. Britain exploded its first nuclear bomb on October 3, 1952.

France, 1960

Why Build the Bomb?

France's memory of World War II was even more powerful than Britain's. It had been an occupied and humiliated country. Most important, French leaders, especially General de Gaulle, who really propelled France into its nuclear-weapons programs in the late 1950s, did not trust other countries to guarantee French security. General de Gaulle repeatedly said that the decision to use nuclear weapons was so grave that no nation would take it to defend another. The French thought the United States had let them down in Vietnam, Algeria, and Egypt in the 1950s, and could not be counted on to stand by its allies.

Another rationale for building the bomb focused on France's role in postwar Europe. The French resented Anglo-American collaboration on nuclear matters in the 1950s and wanted a voice at least equal to Britain's in NATO affairs. In France's view, Britain was too close to America and too far removed from common European security concerns. In the 1960s, after the fact, French officials argued that their nuclear-weapons program would help to counter West German economic dominance of the Common Market by guaranteeing continued French preeminence in scientific and technical achievements.

The French have been less reticent about threatening to destroy cities than other nuclear powers have been; in fact, they have usually seen that threat as the very surest deterrent. Why would the Soviets risk the destruction of Moscow and Leningrad for the conquest of France? French military planners argue, for example, that the ability to destroy even a small number of Soviet cities--to "tear off an arm"--is a sufficient deterrent. There is a much stronger political consensus in France behind the French nuclear *force de dissuasion* than in Britain or the United States.

Who Helped?

Like the British, French physicists had made many of the important discoveries about fission and had helped in the American effort to produce the bomb. Even if the U.S. would not share its knowledge, the French knew what they needed to know. In fact, Szilard said of his French colleague Frederic Joliot-Curie, the father of the French atomic bomb, "If his work had not been interrupted [by the war] he might have beaten us to it." The French exploded their first atomic bomb on February 13, 1960. Israeli scientists are widely believed to have helped in the French bomb project, under the aegis of nuclear cooperation agreements the two countries signed in the mid-fifties.

Notes

A contemporary comment on Joliot-Curie suggests another version of the national prestige rationale for building the bomb: "He wanted to change France's reputation for just nice women's fashions and the niceties of life."

People's Republic of China, 1964

Why Build the Bomb?

The United States had threatened China with nuclear attack twice during the 1950s: once during the Korean War and once during the 1958 crisis over Quemoy and Matsu islands. Although China enjoyed the protection of the Soviet Union, it could make the same argument France had, namely, that no state would risk using nuclear weapons to defend another.

China's case is unique in having had a mid-course reversal about what enemy the bomb is meant to deter. Though the Chinese originally sought the bomb as a deterrent against American threats, they became alarmed about the intentions of the Soviet Union when Sino-Soviet relations deteriorated in the late 1950s. In fact, the Chinese developed two types of intermediate-range missiles capable of striking Moscow before they undertook a serious intercontinental missile program. Since the People's Republic of China was excluded from the United Nations in favor of Nationalist China during this era, international prestige may have been seen as an additional benefit of building the bomb.

Who Helped?

China claimed to have developed nuclear weapons entirely on its own, although some Soviet sources assert that Russian scientists helped their Chinese counterparts early on, and indeed stopped just short of giving them a sample bomb for study purposes. In the wake of China's falling out with the Soviets there were some indirect references to a 1957 nuclear cooperation agreement with the Soviet Union. China claimed in 1963 that the Soviets had not lived up to the terms of the agreement and that all Soviet aid had been withdrawn between 1959 and 1960. The Soviet withdrawal slowed China down, but not for long: The first Chinese bomb was exploded on October 16, 1964.

Notes

China tested its first nuclear device on the very day that Mao's adversary Khruschev fell from power in the Soviet Union, which must have made the Chairman very happy.

5

DE FACTO NUCLEAR
CLUB MEMBERS:
INDIA, ISRAEL, SOUTH AFRICA,
AND PAKISTAN

The door of the Nuclear Club is a wide, gray portal. If we limit manifest club membership to the five acknowledged nuclear-weapons states, we might consider "associate memberships" for India, Israel, South Africa, and Pakistan. All are latent club members in the sense of being "present and capable of becoming though not now visible or active," though only India has conducted a nuclear test. All but Pakistan began nuclear research programs in the late 1940s in the aftermath of World War II, India and Israel within their first year as independent nation-states. Two of the four, India and Pakistan, may be driving each other toward a major nuclear arms race, having fought two conventional wars against each other since 1948. The other two, Israel and South Africa, are both somewhat isolated on the world stage and have allegedly helped each other out on the technological front.

India

Why Build the Bomb?

In the 1960s, China posed a more menacing threat to Indian security than Pakistan did. In November 1962, the Chinese dealt the Indian army a crushing defeat in a Himalayan border war. In the face of that blow and rumors that China would soon test an atomic bomb, an Indian opposition party leader pressed the government of prime minister Nehru to match China's nuclear initiative. Nehru had earlier denied that India would ever build nuclear weapons and refused to entertain the opposition's demand. Nehru died in 1964; six months later China detonated its first atomic bomb. By the end of the year, the new Indian prime minister was implying that India would pursue nuclear explosives for peaceful purposes.

During the 1965 war between India and Pakistan, China threatened to open a second front by attacking India. In 1966, the Indian prime minister died, the United States cut off military aid to India, and China tested a nuclear missile. India's new prime minister, Indira Gandhi, was thus under great pressure to build the bomb, but made no public declaration of her intent until her 1971 statement that India would produce "peaceful nuclear explosions."

In May 1974, India detonated a plutonium device about the size of the bomb that destroyed Hiroshima.

India's "nuclear device" may not have been a deliverable bomb. It might have been too unwieldy in size. But if the Indians can make a big one they can eventually make a small one. Whether it will do so is a question to be taken up by the government of the new prime minister, Rajiv Gandhi, who took his mother's place after she was assassinated in October 1984. He stated early on that India would not build bombs, but the strength of that position could depend on what success Pakistan has with building bombs and how relations on the subcontinent go over the next few years.

Who Helped?

In 1956, Canada sold India a large research reactor for which the United States agreed to supply heavy water. India agreed to use the reactor and any plutonium it produced for peaceful purposes, but would not allow any inspection to ensure that this promise was being kept. The reactor, called CIRUS (Canadian-Indian-Reactor-U.S.), was finished in 1960. In 1962, West Germany sold India a heavy water plant that would be able to replace any heavy water lost at CIRUS. In a 1963 agreement, the United States pledged to help build a pair of reactors at Tarapur. Canada built two more in Rajasthan (all four of these reactors were to be under IAEA safeguards).

India had long opposed international inspection of its nuclear program, declaring that plutonium was integral to its long-term civilian energy plan, which called for plutonium-fueled breeder reactors. The plan thus also required reprocessing capabilities, and American and French firms helped build a reprocessing plant, which was completed in 1966. During the mid-fifties, the United States and France had published formerly classified information on reprocessing, on the rationale that it was critical to any civilian nuclear power program. As part of the Atoms for Peace program, the United States trained 271 foreigners, including 58 Indians, in the techniques of handling plutonium. Thus by 1960 there was an indigenous body of experts capable of dealing with the plutonium produced by CIRUS, which was later used in the core of the 1974 nuclear device.

Four days after that test, Canada cut off all aid to India for the Rajasthan reactors and associated heavy water plant, then under construction. Canada insisted that India put all its nuclear plants under the IAEA safeguards system, and when India refused Canada broke off all preexisting agreements.

The American reaction was considerably milder. A month after the test, the AEC allowed a previously scheduled fuel shipment to go to the Tarapur reactors. The U.S. demanded assurance that the Tarapur plutonium would not be used for any kind of nuclear explosive, however peaceful. For the next few months India would not make any such promises, so the U.S. refused to send more fuel. In September 1974, India agreed, and fuel shipments resumed. The U.S. made no inquiries about Indian plans for use of the plutonium produced by CIRUS.

America's earlier and unwitting complicity in India's pursuit of the bomb may have conditioned the U.S. response. According to former Senator Henry Jackson, India had tried to test a bomb three months before its successful attempt, but it fizzled instead of exploding. Jackson said that the U.S. military had picked up the earlier attempt on seismic detectors, but that the government did not try to talk India out of another attempt. Nor did the government take any measures to impose sanctions after the fact. The accuracy of Jackson's allegations may be questionable, but American response on the financial front is less so. A month after India's successful test, the United States played a leading role in getting a group of Western nations to grant India a $200 million increase in economic aid.

India and the Soviet Union had concluded an alliance in 1971, and there was no public Soviet response to the Indian test. Presumably a nuclear-armed India seemed useful to the Soviets. With their extreme fear of being encircled by enemies, they might have drawn comfort from the notion of having a potential nuclear ally along China's opposite border.

Notes

Indian defense establishment figures have been outspoken in their criticism of the nuclear non-proliferation regime as a discriminatory attempt to keep the Nuclear Club exclusive. K. Subrahmanyam, director of a leading Indian think tank, the Institute for Defense Study and Analysis, presented that argument rather heatedly in a 1984 interview:

The Nuclear Non-Proliferation Treaty perhaps is the greatest impediment today for nuclear disarmament and arms control because that treaty is not what its title implies. It was not to stop proliferation. It was intended actually to extract from an unwary international community a declaration that nuclear weapons are legitimate in the hands of the five nuclear powers...I don't think it is the business of the United States or, for that matter, any other country in the world. If all countries of the world agree not to have nuclear arsenals, then, of course, a country would have the right to tell another country, 'You should not have it.'

However hard it may be for Nuclear Club members to face this kind of criticism, it's an argument that any of the ten countries considered in this chapter or the next could make.

Israel

Why Build the Bomb?

Since 1948, Israel has fought three wars against hostile neighbors, some of whom still will not even concede its right to exist. Security is clearly of paramount concern to Israel.

Who Helped?

Israel provides a useful case study in how a determined would-be nuclear power can get its hands on the right stuff with a little help from its friends, in this case France and the United States.

In 1953, France and Israel signed a nuclear cooperation agreement which was made public the following year.

The French helped Israel build a large research reactor at Dimona in the Negev desert, completed in 1963 or 1964 and capable of producing enough plutonium for one or two bombs a year. Initial work on the plant was kept secret, as was the 1957 resignation of six of the seven members of the Israeli Atomic Energy Commission, apparently in protest against their government's nuclear policy. After a U.S. spy plane reportedly spotted the Dimona plant in 1960, then prime minister David Ben-Gurion publicly announced its existence, declaring that it would be used only for peaceful pursuits such as training and research.

Meanwhile, French-Israeli cooperation increased. A French corporation reportedly helped Israel build a reprocessing plant to separate the plutonium in the spent fuel produced at the Dimona reactor. France may also have reprocessed some of Dimona's spent fuel in exchange for a share of the plutonium. France and Israel allegedly worked together on Israel's Jericho guided missile, which, with a 260-mile range, could deliver a nuclear warhead to many targets in the Middle East. Israeli physicists are said to have helped France develop its nuclear weapons and may have learned enough from that collaboration to forego an Israeli nuclear weapons test.

In order to produce quantities of plutonium at Dimona, Israel needed more uranium than was being processed from the Negev desert deposits. A clandestine nuclear power cannot buy uranium on the open market without drawing attention to itself, so Israel reportedly arranged a heist. In November 1968, Israeli agents allegedly caused some 200 tons of yellowcake (processed uranium ore) to disappear from a ship in the Mediterranean, on its way from Antwerp to Genoa.

As a French diplomat once said rather ruefully to an American proliferation specialist, "Every country has its own sin: you have Britain, Russia has China, and we have Israel." Yet the U.S. cannot claim to be entirely blameless in the case of Israel. The Israelis may have made their plutonium with help from France, but they got their enriched uranium through unofficial American connivance.

The facts of the matter are still in dispute, but the evidence suggests covert aid to the Israeli nuclear-weapons program by private citizens, as well as a blind eye cast on the matter after the fact by the American government.

In 1965, U.S. Atomic Energy Commission investigators discovered during a routine inventory at the NUMEC nuclear fuel fabrication plant in Apollo, Pennsylvania, that 194 pounds of enriched uranium were missing. It takes about 30 pounds to make an atomic bomb, and no audit had ever come up this short before.

AEC officials questioned the plant owner, who at first claimed that the missing uranium had accidentally been buried along with the nuclear waste. After some months of pushing, the AEC forced a showdown and got the wastes exhumed: They found 16 pounds of enriched uranium.

Several months later the AEC conducted another inventory and came up 382 pounds short. The plant management offered another explanation: The missing uranium had somehow leached out into the river. One government official snorted that this hypothesis would presume that the plant had been running full tilt since the Revolutionary War.

The AEC chief investigator was writing a reportedly "blistering" critique of NUMEC's operations when he suddenly left AEC to take a job offered by NUMEC officials.

Early in 1966, the Congressional Joint Committee on Atomic Energy met behind closed doors with AEC officials. The next day, at the request of the committee, the AEC asked the Justice Department to conduct an investigation into the missing NUMEC uranium. After a nine-day investigation, the Justice Department curtly responded that it had determined that there had been no theft, and closed the case. Allegations are that the Johnson White House curtailed the investigation.

According to a CIA theory, the plant had managed to hide its discrepancies for some time by keeping a double set of books. Whatever theory is correct, the fact remains that some 400 pounds of enriched uranium are missing. The plant's owner had close business and government-level ties with Israel, and a case can be made that the missing uranium--or a good portion of it--ended up in the Negev desert. Even if half of what is missing ended up in the river, there's enough left for a handful of atomic bombs.

Notes

Israel has repeatedly said that it will not be the first to introduce nuclear weapons into the Middle East. But it is widely believed to have bomb components that could be assembled into weapons within a few hours. *TIME* magazine reported that Israel had armed a dozen bombs during the 1973 Middle East war. By 1976, the CIA believed Israel to have ten to twenty bombs equal in size to the one that destroyed Hiroshima. Israel could have more than a hundred nuclear weapons in its arsenal by the end of the century, according to a recent study by Georgetown University's Center for Strategic and International Studies.

In fact, a May 1985 *Aerospace Daily* article suggests that the Israelis may already have a highly diversified nuclear force that mirrors in character, albeit not in size, the battlefield and strategic nuclear arsenals of the acknowledged nuclear powers. This report points out that the Israelis probably are capable of delivering nuclear weapons with artillery shells, with Jericho missiles deployed in blast-hardened shelters and caves, and with F-4, F-15, and F-16 aircraft.

Part of the difficulty with this question, not only in the case of Israel, is that nuclear weapons capability is not a fine line that one crosses on a certain date. The sequence of events leading up to the production of a bomb need not necessarily take place in the order we find most logical, i.e., decision, technology, materials, assembly, test. The test shot has been the most common criterion for a country's having crossed the line. For example, Sweden acknowledged early in 1985 that it had conducted nuclear technology tests which included the detonation of a bomb-like device containing shaped high explosives, a small amount of plutonium, and a triggering device. Thus, it may be possible to dispense with an actual test. One can, as many believe Israel does, not even technically "have the bomb," and still be only a matter of hours away from assembling one.

In any case, there is a fair probability that Israel has gotten the advice of outside experts as to whether its devices will work. If this is so, there is less need for a test shot, which would give away the game and further inflame the passions of its hostile neighbors.

South Africa

Why Build the Bomb?

Like Israel, South Africa is isolated and threatened by hostile neighbors against whom it may have to fight to defend its very survival as a nation. Getting the bomb is clearly one way to deter any future military adventures by nations, African or other, who find South African racial policies appalling.

Who Helped?

The United States used South African uranium to produce its nuclear weapons in the years before uranium deposits were discovered in America. In 1957, the United States and South Africa signed a nuclear cooperation agreement, under which nearly one hundred South Africans were to be trained in nuclear technologies at American colleges over the next thirteen years. In the late 1950s, the U.S. allowed South African technicians to monitor some American nuclear test explosions. In 1977, the president of South Africa's Atomic Energy Board acknowledged how useful U.S. training had been: "We can ascribe our degree of advancement today in large measure to training and assistance so willingly provided by the United States of America during the early years of our nuclear program when several of the Western nations cooperated in initiating our scientists and engineers into nuclear science." Under the same agreement, the United States sold South Africa a research reactor, SAFARI I, which was completed in 1965 and brought under IAEA safeguards in 1967.

In 1970, South Africa announced that it had perfected a new uranium enrichment process. The process has been kept secret, but is reported to be similar to an aerodynamic technique called the Becker nozzle, developed in West Germany. The West German government forbade the German firm that developed the technology to work with South Africa, but the company is reported to have covertly helped South Africa build an enrichment plant at Valindaba. Since South Africa ostensibly built the plant on its own, IAEA safeguards do not apply.

Other countries have assisted South Africa's nuclear effort as well. Britain may have transferred the technology for producing uranium hexafluoride to South Africa in 1965, and German, French, Swiss, and American firms have made substantial sales to the South African nuclear program, some of which would now be outlawed by the Non-Proliferation Treaty and Suppliers Guidelines which did not exist then. In 1973, the U.S. Commerce Department let a computer firm sell specially modified computers to South Africa for use at its Valindaba enrichment plant, without checking with any of the agencies that purportedly control proliferation policy and sales of sensitive technology. The Valindaba plant reached full operating capacity in 1977 and reportedly can produce enough enriched uranium for two or three bombs a year.

In mid-1974, the United States signed a greatly expanded nuclear cooperation agreement with South Africa, agreeing to provide enriched uranium for the fuel needed by two reactors to be built at Koeberg. South Africa had agreed to buy the plants from General Electric, but Congressional opposition blocked the sale in 1976, so South Africa bought them from France instead. The fuel arrangement remained intact, however, even though Congressional pressure had forced the Ford administration to suspend fuel shipments to SAFARI I in 1975.

The shift in U.S. policy serves to illustrate how a state determined to get the bomb can take advantage of the loopholes in the non-proliferation system and the complicity of nuclear suppliers in order to make headway. Because South Africa refuses to sign the Non-Proliferation Treaty or to allow international inspectors into its uranium enrichment plant, the U.S. government in 1977 refused to send back a shipment of uranium that South Africa had paid the Department of Energy to enrich. The U.S. government also got France to agree not to fabricate enriched uranium fuel elements for South Africa, unless it agreed to sign the treaty and allow international inspections.

South Africa came under a good deal of pressure in the early 1980s because its Koeberg nuclear power station was close to completion. The first reactor went into operation in 1984 and the second is scheduled to start up in 1985. While the Valindaba enrichment plant can produce enough enriched uranium for several bombs a year, it is a pilot project and cannot produce enough to fuel the reactors. Producing electricity requires a good deal more nuclear fuel than producing bombs does.

The United States had since changed its stance on the matter. According to a State Department official, we "feel that we can achieve our [nonproliferation] goals better with South Africa by not engaging in unnecessary actions which would produce a deteriorating relation." This new approach is called "constructive engagement." Under constructive engagement, the U.S. government let American brokers arrange for South African fuel purchases from Belgium and Switzerland and has gone along with France's willingness to fabricate the fuel into rods.

In 1982, the chairman of the House Subcommittee on African Affairs questioned an assistant secretary of state about this policy. Specifically, he wanted to know whether the U.S. had tried to discourage France from honoring its contract to fabricate fuel.

Assistant Secretary: We discussed this with the government of France and told them what our position was. They told us what they intend to do. They were not going to breach a contract they concluded with South Africa in the mid-seventies, quite frankly.

Subcommittee Chairman: Did we ask them to?

Assistant Secretary: Well, the word 'ask' has different meanings.

Subcommittee Chairman: Suggest? Hint? Intimate?

Assistant Secretary: I'm not sure I would want to characterize it that way.

The chairman concluded that the way the matter was handled came "dangerously close to compromising the nuclear non-proliferation policies of the United States."

In addition the Koeberg complex may be getting un-official, even illegal, help from American citizens. Early in 1985, American nuclear reactor operators were reported to be working at the plant, in violation of a 1983 U.S. law requiring prior official permission to do so. The Americans, who were allegedly former employees of the Tennessee Valley Authority, were apparently lured to South Africa by the offer of $100,000 annual salaries, free housing, and other benefits. (Reactor operator salaries at TVA range from $31,000 to $52,000 a year.) Workers who took jobs in South Africa before the 1983 law was passed may be immune from prosecution, but the eleven operators who reportedly went to work in South Africa in 1984 could face a maximum penalty of ten years in prison and a $10,000 fine. There have been Congressional alle-gations that the Department of Energy knew about the case for a year before it appeared in the press, but DOE officials, like those at the State Department, claim they heard about it only late in 1984.

South Africa is constructing a commercial-scale uranium enrichment plant twenty to thirty times the size of its Valindaba plant, ostensibly to make fuel for its power reactors. Pretoria has said that it may be willing to put the new plant under IAEA safeguards, which would make it more difficult to divert nuclear material without detection.

Still, its refusal to place safeguards on the exist-ing Valindaba plant and veiled hints by some officials lead most observers to believe that South Africa has stockpiled enough nuclear material for fifteen to twenty-five nuclear bombs which could be assembled in a short time.

Notes

South Africa also provides a case study of U.S.-Soviet cooperation on non-proliferation. In 1977 a So-viet spy satellite spotted a nuclear test site in South Africa's Kalahari Desert. The American analysts who pore over satellite photoreconnaissance images had missed the tell-tale signs and thus never ordered up the second set of pictures with a higher resolution that "zoom lens" satellites can supply. When the Soviets told the U.S.

about the site on August 6, American analysts went looking for it and confirmed the Soviet find.

The United States immediately went to work, along with France, Britain, and West Germany, in an attempt to muscle South Africa into foregoing a nuclear test. The joint effort reportedly included a French threat to block completion of the Koeberg reactors and a threatened break in diplomatic relations by a number of other Western governments. This concerted action to avert the immediate danger of a South African nuclear test was successful, and within two weeks President Carter announced that "South Africa has informed us that they do not intend to develop nuclear explosive devices for any purpose, either peaceful or as a weapon, that the Kalahari test site which has been in question is not designed for the use of nuclear explosives, and that no nuclear explosive test will be taken in South Africa now or in the future." But South African Prime Minister John Vorster later denied having made any such promise, while at the same time repeating an assertion that his country is "only interested in peaceful development of nuclear facilities."

Although this joint diplomatic venture did not address the larger question of IAEA safeguards, it did demonstrate that the U.S. and the Soviet Union do share common ground on matters of nuclear proliferation and that they can cooperate when necessary.

South Africa's name also comes up in discussions concerning whether there may have been a nuclear test shot in a remote region of the South Atlantic in 1979, when satellites picked up the characteristic double flash that signals a nuclear explosion. Nobody has claimed it though, and scientific analysis suggests that the flash could have been a natural phenomenon. A White House report claimed that the signal picked up by the satellites was significantly different from that of a nuclear explosion and all but ruled out a nuclear test as the source.

Pakistan

Pakistan probably does not yet have the bomb, but it is much closer to having it than the six countries we call "prospective Nuclear Club members," and discuss in

65

the next chapter. According to Israeli intelligence, by 1986 Pakistan may have ten bombs the size of the one that destroyed Hiroshima. U.S. and Indian estimates are more conservative, but both agree that Pakistan is very close to crossing the nuclear threshold. Who outside Pakistan will know when it has edged across it, given that it is likely to forego a test and opt instead for "bomb in the basement" capacity--the ability to make a weapon on short notice, without testing it?

Why Build the Bomb?

Pakistan and India are traditional enemies, and India has a demonstrated nuclear-explosives capability. After its last defeat by India in 1971, Pakistan lost part of its territory, East Pakistan, which became the nation of Bangladesh. The Indian test probably didn't look like a "peaceful nuclear explosion" to Pakistan. The Soviet invasion of Afghanistan in 1979 was a further blow to Pakistan's sense of security. And the Pakistanis haven't enhanced their security by becoming a conduit for American arms on their way to the Afghan rebels.

Pakistan also aspires to a position of leadership in the Moslem world. Former Prime Minister Bhutto (later executed by the current regime) laid bare this motive in chilling terms: "Christian, Jewish, and Hindu civilizations have this [nuclear] capability. The Communist powers also possess it. Only the Islamic civilization is without it. But that position is about to change.... We will eat grass or leaves, even go hungry, but we will get one of our own."

Who Helped?

Pakistan has received more outside help from more countries more recently than any of the other de facto nuclear powers, which makes it a particularly useful study in evaluating how effective the nuclear non-proliferation regime has been up to the present. We will thus consider Pakistan's nuclear weapons program in greater detail than those of India, Israel, or South Africa.

Pakistan established its Atomic Energy Committee in 1955, and in the decade that followed 37 Pakistani scientists were trained in the United States. Pakistan's first research reactor, bought from the United States and placed under IAEA safeguards, went into operation in 1965. Except for providing training, that reactor has not contributed to Pakistan's nuclear-weapons program.

In 1972, Pakistan's first nuclear power plant, called KANUPP, was completed. Canada built it, supplied the fuel and, along with the United States, supplied the heavy water. At about the same time, Pakistan acquired a small, British-designed reprocessing plant, useful mainly for training scientists in handling plutonium, since its plutonium output is insignificant.

In the early 1970s, Pakistan got nearly a billion dollars in grants and loans from Arab countries and Iran, thus sharing in the new-found wealth of these oil-producing states. Then Prime Minister Bhutto was particularly close to Libya's Colonel Qaddafi, who reportedly agreed to fund Pakistan's nuclear weapons program.

In October 1974, a French firm agreed to build a large commercial-scale reprocessing plant at Chashma, able to process more than five times the yearly output of the Canadian-built KANUPP reactor. Pakistan also enlisted the help of the same French firm and a Belgian firm to build a smaller, secret reprocessing plant, called New Labs, which when activated would be able to produce enough plutonium for two to four nuclear weapons a year.

Pakistan had a strategy for highly enriched uranium as well. Dr. Abdul Qadir Khan, a Pakistani engineer who had studied in Holland and Belgium for ten years, worked at a Dutch engineering firm between 1972 and 1975. He spirited highly classified blueprints for an ultracentrifuge uranium enrichment plant out of the Netherlands, along with a detailed list of necessary equipment. Pakistan was already shopping from the list even before Khan left his job in Holland. He later directed construction of a plant with thousands of centrifuges near Kahuta, a plant that was later named after him.

After the Indian test in 1974, the United States grew more concerned about proliferation and tried to persuade Pakistan and France to cancel the Chasma reprocessing plant contract. Secretary of State Kissinger shuttled between Islamabad and Paris, but his counsel fell on deaf ears in both capitals. French president Valery Giscard d'Estaing announced in December 1976 that France would sell no more reprocessing plants until further notice, but that policy did not apply to the preexisting deal with Pakistan.

The deal went forward for a while, but when the United States came up with new evidence of Pakistan's nuclear weapons ambitions, France began balking, calling a work slowdown of sorts, in the hope that Pakistan would call off the agreement. The Carter administration cut off military and economic aid to Pakistan in September 1977 because it refused to stop pursuing completion of the French plant.

A year later France reneged on the contract, and U.S. aid to Pakistan was restored. Workers from the French firm kept helping Pakistan all through 1979, and when they stopped in 1980 Pakistan tried to continue on its own, using French blueprints. It was clear that President Zia (who deposed Bhutto in 1977) intended to pursue the bomb as vigorously as his predecessor had.

Meanwhile, the Pakistanis had been working steadily on their enrichment plant at Kahuta and their secret New Labs reprocessing plant. Swiss, British, and Dutch firms sold them items that, while not on the Nuclear Suppliers Group "trigger list," were highly suspect. Six thousand specially hardened steel cases for centrifuges caught the Dutch government's attention, but the sale went ahead anyway.

In accordance with provisions of U.S. law, U.S. aid was cut off again in April 1979, when it was determined that Pakistan had received specially designed uranium enrichment from abroad. At that time, there were press reports that the U.S. contemplated covert military action against the Pakistani uranium-enrichment plant, but U.S. officials denied them.

The Soviet invasion of Afghanistan on December 25, 1979, turned around U.S. policy toward Pakistan. In response to the invasion, the Carter administration proposed a $400-million aid package for Pakistan. President Zia dismissed this offer as "peanuts"; he wanted more money and a formal security guarantee instead. Discussions on how much aid and how formal a security guarantee continued all through 1980, but the Soviet presence in Afghanistan decidedly softened the tenor of U.S. policy toward Pakistan. In 1981, the U.S. and Pakistan agreed on a six-year, $3.2-billion security-assistance package, which included the outright sale of 40 F-16 aircraft to Pakistan.

The Libyan connection came into play again in 1979 - 80 when Libya bought several hundred tons of yellowcake (processed uranium) from Niger and reportedly passed it along to Pakistan. Although Libya had signed the NPT, the IAEA monitoring program for Libya was not yet set up, so the sale slipped through the gap.

During the same years, French, Swiss, and Belgian firms allegedly supplied items needed for the Khan centrifuge plant at Kahuta and the New Labs reprocessing plant. A West German firm illegally supplied the facility for turning yellowcake into uranium hexafluoride, the feed material for a gas centrifuge enrichment plant. In 1980, Pakistan announced that it had achieved the ability to fabricate fuel elements for use in the KANUPP reactors. Canada had cut off all nuclear aid to Pakistan in 1976 because Pakistan would not accept IAEA safeguards on all its installations; by 1980 Pakistan had its own fuel-fabrication plant and was no longer dependent on outside suppliers.

Another development in 1980 was the arrest in Canada of three Pakistani men, one the owner of a Montreal electrical supply store and the other two electrical engineers, who were sending Pakistan items that would be useful in completing its centrifuge plant. Two Montreal electrical supply shops had bought the parts from General Electric, Westinghouse, RCA, and Motorola and then re-packed them for shipment to Pakistan. The Mounties seized nineteen crates of equipment awaiting shipment to Pakistan, but ten crates had already been sent. At the trial, which ended in the summer of 1984, the defendants were able to convince the jury that the parts were for such innocuous enterprises as a textile plant, a food processing plant, and á synthetic butter factory. One was acquitted and the other two drew small fines on minor charges.

In the meantime, the Reagan administration tried to dissuade Pakistan from pursuing the bomb. The U.S. in 1981 offered President Zia aid at a much higher level than President Carter had offered: a six-year, $3.2 billion package, to include forty F-16 aircraft. The intent was to persuade Pakistan that nuclear weapons are not in its best interest, and Congress attached a rider to the aid package stating that a nuclear-weapons test would end all aid.

Several revelations in 1981 implied that Pakistan had not been turned away from the nuclear weapons path. A test site was allegedly under construction in the mountains near the Afghanistan border. A Pakistani army colonel was arrested at Kennedy Airport in New York City for trying to smuggle zirconium (the metal used in constructing fuel rods) out of the country. Late in 1981, the IAEA announced that it could no longer certify that spent nuclear fuel was not being diverted from certain kinds of nuclear reactors because of deficiencies in the safeguards system for those reactors. Pakistan's KANUPP reactor fell into this category, and Pakistan's announcement the previous year that it was fabricating and introducing its own fuel elements into the KANUPP reactor further complicated the problem. Negotiations on improving IAEA monitoring equipment at KANUPP lasted more than a year, and it was only in March 1983 that the Agency was again sure that its safeguards were working.

In 1982, the Reagan administration tightened the no-nuclear-test rule made explicit in its aid, and implied to Pakistan that even reprocessing to produce plutonium would jeopardize continued aid.

All during 1983 Pakistan tried to get a nuclear supplier country to agree to build a large nuclear power plant at Chashma, without success. U.S. firms were prohibited from bidding on the proposed plant by the Nuclear Non-Proliferation Act (since Pakistan would not put all its nuclear installations under IAEA safeguards), but there was some worry that France or Germany might offer a deal, especially since nuclear business was bad. Whether the reason was Pakistan's manifest nuclear ambitions or its lack of cash, the nuclear supplier nations for once presented a united front in refusing to build the reactor.

In February 1984, Dr. Khan, director of Pakistan's centrifuge plant, announced that "by the grace of God, Pakistan is now among the few countries that can efficiently enrich uranium." Dr. Khan enlarged on his theme in a report published in a scholarly Pakistani journal: "Such an achievement by our team in a country where no basic infrastructure is available, where we cannot make a good bicycle or even a grinding machine, speaks [for] itself." President Zia toned down that exuberance a bit some weeks later when he referred to Pakistan's "very modest research and development capability of uranium enrichment." In June, Senator Alan Cranston reported that Pakistan had finished a thousand centrifuge units, enough to produce the enriched uranium for one well-designed weapon a year. U.S. intelligence reports are more skeptical, claiming that the enrichment effort has been slowed by centrifuge breakdowns and that the plant itself was seriously damaged by an earthquake in late 1983. Chinese technicians have been spotted at the site and are believed to be helping with repair work.

Pakistan has also been working on weapon design problems. China has allegedly helped Pakistan with the design of a nuclear weapon, and may have given Pakistan the design for the bomb used in its own 1966 nuclear test in exchange for information about centrifuge enrichment technology.

Canadian prosecutors were embarrassed at their failure to convict the three Pakistanis caught smuggling items useful for centrifuge enrichment out of Canada in 1980. America has equal grounds for chagrin over the case of Nazir Ahmed Vaid, a Pakistani businessman--or agent, depending on what version of the facts one accepts. Vaid was arrested in Houston in the summer of 1984 for trying to smuggle krytrons (devices used to trigger nuclear bombs) out of the country. U.S. attorneys, and even the judge who heard the case and passed sentence, seem to have overlooked the connection between the defendant and the director of procurement for Pakistan's Atomic Energy Commission, even though letters linking the two had been seized by customs agents. Vaid was allowed to plea bargain and was deported after being convicted on a minor charge.

Notes

A Pakistani nuclear test would probably compel India to produce nuclear devices that are assuredly not "peaceful." If history is a guide, the two countries could find themselves facing off yet again, this time both armed with atomic bombs. The alliance structure here does not inspire confidence: The Soviets support India, the United States and China support Pakistan. If India and Pakistan had a nuclear war, what would their sponsors do?

Given that Pakistan is unlikely to conduct a test during the period when U.S. security assistance is being provided, a more plausible near-term worry is that of conventional air attack on its nuclear installations, either by India in order to preserve its status as the only nuclear power on the subcontinent or by Israel out of fear that an "Islamic" bomb might be shared with such hostile states as Libya.

Plotting Against Time--and the Bomb

How far back should we step if we want a proper view of how we're doing, set against the permanence of the nuclear age and the fact that we're only forty years into it? We are the generation on the cusp of that age--stewards of a planet with billions of generations of life left in it.

Can we plot a curve and see some trends--look beyond the simple statistics of the nine that have made it into the nuclear club in the first forty years and give our-selves a better grade than that sobering statistic im-plies? The charts below show two ways to look at this progression. You can probably think of others. Give us a grade--and then decide who really earned it.

Two Different Ways
to Look at the Growth
in the Nuclear Club

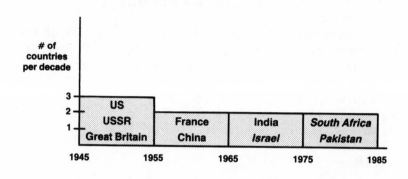

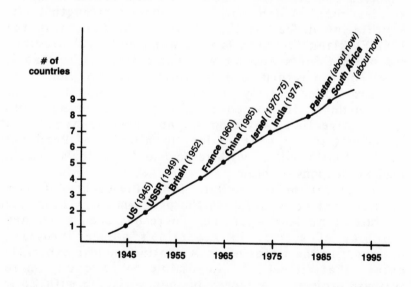

Artwork, Michelle Higgins

73

6

PROSPECTIVE NUCLEAR CLUB MEMBERS: ARGENTINA, BRAZIL, IRAQ, LIBYA, SOUTH KOREA, AND TAIWAN

We have seen why and how the manifest and de facto Nuclear Club members got the bomb. It is useful to consider--in specifics for each country that follows-- whether this group of nations nearing Nuclear Club membership will be deterred from building the bomb by the arguments and deterrents that failed to dissuade the countries that already have it.

Argentina

Why Build the Bomb?

Argentina's rivalry with Brazil for hegemony in South America and its wish to follow its own course in world affairs require demonstrable military strength. Its humiliating defeat at the hands of the British in the 1982 Falkland/Malvinas Islands war could have provided the pretext for a nuclear weapons drive, but instead it resulted in a return to democratic, civilian rule. That war also added greatly to Argentina's already enormous foreign debt. Its consequent financial crisis may help to turn Argentina away from the nuclear-weapons path. It is too soon to say what the long-term policy of President Raul Alfonsin will be with respect to Argentina's nascent nuclear weapons program.

On taking office in late 1983, President Alfonsin implied that he would turn the program away from the pursuit of nuclear weapons. There has been a decided lessening of secrecy in Argentina's nuclear program, designed, in the words of an Argentine nuclear expert, to ensure that "it will be impossible to have any more surprise projects." A thorny boundary dispute with Chile over the Beagle channel has also been resolved through Papal mediation.

Argentina's experience of internal political violence over the past thirty years--six of eleven presidents

74

deposed in coups and the "disappearance" of thousands of Argentines during the last military junta's rule--might dissuade it from building the bomb, since it could fall into the hands of extremists at home.

Another reason to forego the bomb is that Argentina could not hope to be the only nuclear power in South America for long: Brazil would soon follow suit, and possibly Chile as well.

Who Helped / Is Helping?

Argentina's nuclear program got off to an inauspicious start when in 1951 an Argentine scientist who had formerly worked for Hitler's Third Reich claimed a successful controlled fusion experiment, later proved to be a hoax.

In 1955, Argentina and the United States signed a nuclear cooperation agreement under which Argentina used a U.S. design to build its first research reactor. By 1967, Argentina had built three more research reactors on its own. All of them, as well as a German-made research reactor completed in 1972, were under IAEA safeguards because their equipment, highly enriched uranium fuel, or both came from the United States, and the U.S. had made application of such safeguards a condition of supply.

In 1968, Argentina bought a power reactor called Atucha I from West Germany. The Atucha I reactor can be refueled without shutting down, which makes it more difficult to safeguard. The United States supplied heavy water for the plant and, until the mid-1980s, West Germany made its fuel rods using native Argentine uranium. Argentina tried to limit IAEA safeguards on the reactor to five years, but its need for U.S. heavy water and West German fuel rods forced it to back down.

Argentina tried again to limit IAEA safeguards in a 1972 agreement with Canada to buy a nuclear power plant. Canada reportedly agreed to a fifteen-year limit on IAEA safeguards, but in the aftermath of India's 1974 nuclear test thought differently about the matter and got Argentina to accept extended safeguards on the plant.

When the military government came to power in 1976, it stepped up Argentine efforts. In 1969 Argentina had built a laboratory-scale reprocessing plant near the Buenos Aires airport at Ezeiza. In 1977, possibly with

help from Italy, Argentina began building a larger reprocessing plant at Ezeiza.

Late in 1983, just before President Alfonsin was
inaugurated, Argentina announced that it had been secretly building a gaseous diffusion uranium enrichment plant
at Pilcaniyeu over the previous five years. Argentina
maintains that the products from this plant will be used
in its nuclear power program and as exports. However, it
should be noted that there will be no safeguards and the
plant's capacity seems many times larger than Argentina's
nuclear power program should require. The reprocessing
plant begun near Buenos Aires in 1977 is due to be finished in 1986, and the Congressional Research Service
estimates that it will have the capacity to produce
enough plutonium for about ten atomic bombs a year.
However, that estimate may be a moot point. Argentina
has no access to unsafeguarded fuel, so the plant will
have to operate under the purview of the IAEA. As noted
above, apparent progress toward the bomb in the period
1978-83 could well be turned around by the new democratic
government.

Argentina has refused to sign the Non-Proliferation
Treaty, arguing, as India does, that the document locks
all the countries which did not have nuclear weapons by
1967 into a state of permanent inferiority, while treat-
ing the "Big Five" as legitimate bomb owners. Argentina
has signed, but not ratified, the 1967 Treaty of Tlate-
lolco, which would ban nuclear weapons in all of Latin
America. Twenty-five other Latin American countries have
signed and ratified the Treaty, but Cuba is a significant
holdout. Most of those who have signed and ratified the
Treaty have agreed to waive the provision that it does
not become binding unless all Latin American countries
are party to it. The only two parties to the treaty
which have not waived that provision are Chile and
Brazil.

Brazil

Why Build the Bomb?

Brazil lags behind Argentina in developing the infrastructure and nuclear materials necessary for serious
pursuit of the bomb. Yet as the biggest, most populous,

and richest country in South America, Brazil may be driven to match Argentine progress on the nuclear front in order to maintain its national prestige.

The manner in which regional rivalry can drive non-nuclear states toward the bomb is evident in the Argentina/Brazil case. The initial Brazilian reaction to the 1983 Argentine announcement of its secret enrichment plant at Pilcaniyeu was mild. Indeed, the Brazilian president sent his peer in Argentina a congratulatory letter. Yet Brazil could not be sanguine about its rival's success; over the following weeks, a number of military officers quoted in the press suggested that Brazil could have nuclear weapons by 1990. Early in 1984, Brazil's navy minister, while denying pursuit of the bomb, made the case for keeping nuclear options open:

...We, the military, are not going after the bomb. With the development of nuclear research, however, one day the country will inevitably have the material necessary to build the bomb. It is a good thing to have that capacity. But just because we possess that capacity, manufacturing the bomb will make no sense because we do not intend to go to war against anyone. Where would we drop the bomb? On our heads? So we will not build any nuclear device.

Like Argentina, Brazil has avoided signing the Non-Proliferation Treaty or becoming bound by the Treaty for the Denuclearization of Latin America, thus ensuring no international scrutiny of its nuclear program, except that demanded by nuclear supplier countries, will come into play. Whether Brazil will exercise its option to build the bomb is a decision that will probably be put off until the 1990s. A civilian government was restored in early 1985, but, as with Argentina, there is no telling whether a civilian government will slow or halt the momentum of an incipient nuclear weapons program. The probable deciding factor in Brazil's future policy will be the Argentine stance on nuclear weapons development.

Who Helped/Is Helping?

Like Argentina, Brazil solicited the aid of a former

Third Reich scientist when it concluded a secret deal in 1953 to buy three experimental ultracentrifuges in West Germany. U.S. occupation forces discovered the deal and blocked it, but after they departed the centrifuges were sent to Brazil.

Brazil signed a nuclear cooperation agreement with the United States in 1955, and in 1957 the U.S. provided a research reactor, dependent on U.S. fuel and therefore subject to IAEA safeguards, as well as two other research reactors completed in 1965, also under agency safeguards.

After an earlier deal with France fell through, Brazil bought a nuclear power plant called Angra I from the United States in 1971. Since at the time Brazil thought that it lacked significant native uranium deposits, the independence from U.S.-supplied enriched uranium sought by Argentina was not then an option. The plant was completed in 1982.

Meanwhile, Brazil pursued centrifuge enrichment technology, signing agreements with France and West Germany for joint ventures in this field, apparently without IAEA safeguards.

Brazil signed a nuclear agreement with West Germany in 1975 that could ultimately give it a complete nuclear fuel cycle. Germany agreed to supply two power plants by 1985, with the option of six more by 1990. Germany also offered to help Brazil find native uranium, in exchange for a fifth of the ore. And, to complete the cycle, Germany agreed to supply a fuel fabrication plant and to initiate Brazilian scientists into the mysteries of Becker nozzle enrichment and reprocessing. West Germany demanded IAEA safeguards on all this technology and added secret controls of its own on the rate of delivery. Fuel for the first two reactors in the deal, Angra II and III, was to come from a West German/British/Dutch consortium, with the Dutch exacting an additional safeguard: Any plutonium produced from that fuel had to be stored in a multinational facility or, barring that, returned to the consortium.

Brazil's subsequent nuclear development has suffered from delays and cost overruns, and its mounting financial crisis has forced it to cut back the German deal by 40%, so it may have to make do with only three nuclear power plants. But it is completing its West German-built enrichment plant at Resende and may, by 1990, be able to produce enough enriched uranium to fuel the three plants. Work is also proceeding on a reprocessing plant, expected to go into operation in the late 1980s. The West German-assisted uranium search was so successful that Brazil, which once thought itself poor in uranium, is now ranked seventh in the world in uranium deposits.

More troubling than this progress achieved with outside help is the progress Brazil is making on its own, since no international safeguards can be imposed on it. Plans call for a small ultracentrifuge enrichment plant to be completed by 1987 and a larger model three years later. Already completed is a small plant for making uranium hexafluoride. Laser enrichment technology is also under study. Brazil's first indigenous research reactor is under construction, and if the centrifuge enrichment plant can provide unsafeguarded fuel, Brazil would have access to a source of plutonium useful for any future nuclear weapons program.

A good many other countries have also made nuclear agreements with Brazil, among them France, Argentina, South Africa, and China. Iraq made a deal in 1980 before the destruction of Osirak under which Brazil would trade uranium and technical advice for an (alleged) Iraqi promise that there would be no increase in its oil bill. It probably looked like an offer Brazil couldn't refuse, since nearly half the oil that fueled its entire economy was coming from Iraq. Some eight tons of uranium oxide had been shipped to Iraq before the Israeli raid on Osirak made further shipments moot. It is not known whether, or to what extent, Brazil may have agreed to share its domestically produced technology with Iraq.

Brazil does not now appear to be a serious proliferation threat. It was not always so. The United States and Brazil broke off military ties in 1977 after the U.S. voiced criticism over human rights abuses. The Nuclear Non-Proliferation Act of 1978, which bans nuclear fuel exports to countries that refuse to put all their nuclear facilities under IAEA safeguards, led to a fuel embargo against Brazil. The fuel embargo was relaxed in 1981 when the Reagan administration allowed Brazil to buy fuel elsewhere without the financial penalties its contract called for, and Brazil and the U.S. resumed informal military and industrial cooperation in 1984.

Iraq

Why Build the Bomb?

Iraq is implacable in its hostility to Israel and refuses to recognize its right to exist. As a socialist Arab state, Iraq has been a major exporter of radical politics to the Middle East, as well as oil to the rest of the world, until its war with Iran cut oil production. The bomb thus might look like a way to match the presumed Israeli bomb and at the same time enhance Iraq's leadership role in the Arab world.

Who Helped/Is Helping?

The Soviet Union supplied Iraq with a small research reactor, completed in 1968 at the Tuwaitha Atomic Center. The next year Iraq signed the Non-Proliferation Treaty, and there was little reason to suspect Iraq of harboring nuclear weapons ambitions until 1974.

In 1974, Iraq signed a nuclear cooperation agreement with France, under which France would supply a large reactor and help turn the Tuwaitha Atomic Center into a "nuclear university." What France got from the deal was a promise of oil and a market for French arms merchants.

The sales contract signed in 1976 ultimately promised two reactors (dubbed Osirak and Isis by the French, after the Egyptian god of the underworld and his consort). There was an outcry from the United States, Israel, and several European countries: The highly enriched uranium fuel used in these reactors could be turned directly into nuclear weapons if Iraq chose to ignore IAEA safeguards.

There was also a longer-term proliferation worry. Osirak could produce enough plutonium for perhaps two bombs a year. It was many times bigger than reactors in other developing countries. In 1978, after countries like Saudi Arabia and Syria joined the protest, France tried to offer a less dangerous fuel, enriched to a lower level and thus unsuitable for use in nuclear explosives, but Iraq would accept no substitute.

Throughout 1979 and 1980 there were acts of sabotage against Iraq's program. Key parts for Osirak and Isis were bombed in a French warehouse where they were awaiting shipment to Iraq. Rebuilding their cores took about six months, and though a French environmental group claimed responsibility for the bomb attack, Israeli agents were under suspicion, as was the French government in some quarters. Then an Egyptian nuclear scientist who had come to France to inspect the first fuel shipment was murdered in his Paris hotel room. The murder was never solved, though again Israeli agents were suspected. There was a series of bombings at the homes and plants of Iraq's suppliers: an Italian firm that had sold Iraq hot cells, its partner, and the French firm supplying Osirak. This time suspicion focused on Iran as well as Israel, since there had been threatening letters about protecting the Islamic revolution. In September 1980, eight days after Iraq launched an attack against Iran, Iranian jets attacked Osirak. The damage was not crippling, but it delayed startup for another six months.

In 1980 France finally got Iraq to agree to three conditions that would help prevent possible use of Osirak and its fuel for nuclear weapons. First, France would limit its shipments of highly enriched uranium to one Osirak load and one reload at any given time. The total would still be enough for one nuclear weapon, but Osirak would be using half of it at any time. Second, Iraq would agree to use the small Isis reactor to irradiate all fresh fuel, making it nearly as radioactive as the load in use in Osirak. Radioactive fuel *could* still have been used for weapons, but it would have been hard to do since it poses a mortal threat to workers, who have to be shielded. The first and only shipment (27 1/2 pounds) arrived in July, 1980. France also got Iraq to agree that French technicians could stay on at the reactor until 1989 as supervisors.

As it happened, there was no need to stay on. On June 7, 1981, Israeli jets destroyed Osirak in a surprise bombing raid. After the raid, Iraqi President Saddam Hussein called on all peace-loving nations to "assist the Arabs in one way or another to obtain the nuclear bomb in order to confront Israel's existing bombs." In mid-July, Saudi Arabia agreed to pay for rebuilding Osirak.

France agreed to rebuild the plant, but demanded stricter terms: Iraq would have to accept the less dangerous fuel it had earlier rejected; it would have to include neighboring countries in plans for the plant, making it a regional operation; and French technicians would stay on at the plant permanently. Iraq has not said whether it will accept these conditions. It has said that it will rebuild Osirak, but its attention is of necessity focused on its war with Iran and there has been no work on rebuilding the plant.

Iraq's conduct of that war raises questions about a short-term proliferation threat. Iraq violated the Geneva Protocol by using chemical weapons, including mustard gas, against Iran. This does not inspire confidence in Iraq's compliance with other treaties to which it is party, for instance, the Non-Proliferation Treaty. Iraq still has the 27 1/2 pounds of highly enriched uranium supplied as fuel for Osirak, enough for one well-designed nuclear bomb. If the tide of the war turns in Iran's favor, might Iraq use such a weapon? Who will get his hands on the bomb material if an Iranian victory should lead to extreme political disintegration in Iraq?

The Soviet Union has agreed to build Iraq's first nuclear power plant, which will probably be completed in the mid-1990s. The plant will use low-enriched fuel, not in itself useful for nuclear weapons. Unless the Soviet Union demands the return of spent fuel, however, Iraq might be able to reprocess it for plutonium using its Italian hot cell.

Iraq may have found a quicker route to plutonium. The Italian press reported in 1984 that Iraq was trying to buy plutonium, uranium, and plastic explosives on the Italian black market. Thirty Italians, including a former member of the Italian secret service, were charged with conspiracy in the case. The ringleaders were reportedly arrested before the transaction could go through, but if the Italian allegations are true, there is little doubt that Iraq is still in hot pursuit of the bomb and will not let the rule of law or its signature on the NPT stand in its way.

Notes

The Israeli destruction of Osirak set off a firestorm of protest, and not only from the obvious quarters. Osirak was to have been under IAEA safeguards, and the agency's director publicly claimed that the Israeli raid was nearly as damaging a blow to the safeguards system itself as to Osirak. Why should countries subscribe to the rule of law--the non-proliferation regime--if a vigilante might blow them up anyway?

From an Israeli point of view, the IAEA regime probably looked like a toothless watchdog. Safeguards do not keep fuel safe. They merely determine if anything is amiss and alert the world to it. Timely warning, it's called, and it assumes that the alerted world will then act to stop the cheater from building the bomb. But by the time the watchdog barks, the trail might be cold: The interval between inspections is many times longer than the time it could take to build a bomb from diverted material.

By the time of the IAEA general conference in the fall of 1982, Israel had invaded Lebanon, further fueling the anti-Israeli hostility simmering in many other countries. By a vote of member countries, Israel was denied credentials at the conference. The U.S. walked out in protest, taking with it sixteen other member countries and part of the money it contributes toward IAEA's support.

There followed a period of intense debate within the U.S. government about the worth of the IAEA and where U.S. interests lay. Those who argued for a lasting break thought it crucial that the U.S. should show that it will not countenance the "politicizing" of an independent agency operating under the aegis of the United Nations. Those who thought the U.S. should mend the breach argued that the agency could not do its job without the U.S. dollars that were a substantial part of its budget. The government finally decided that the IAEA was too important to abandon. In early 1983, the U.S. returned, along with some of its missing support payments, after the agency declared that Israel would be allowed to participate fully.

Libya

Why Build the Bomb?

Colonel Muammer el Qaddafi and his socialist regime came to power in Libya in 1969. Qaddafi turned American and British military forces out soon thereafter, and in the early 1970s became a leader in the OPEC struggle against Western oil companies. His subsequent export of international terrorism has earned him and his People's Congresses pariah status in much of the world. Even some Arab states have reason to fear his intemperate hostility, as in 1983 when a People's Congress plot to take over Islam's most holy shrine, the Grand Mosque at Mecca, was rumored. Israel and its main ally, the United States, are the prime targets of his rage, however, and having the bomb would increase enormously the scope of threats or violence open to him.

Who Helped/Is Helping?

Colonel Qaddafi announced in 1975 that Libya would soon have the bomb: "A few years ago we could hardly manage to procure a squadron of fighter planes. Tomorrow, we shall be able to buy an atom bomb." Qaddafi had, in fact, already tried to buy an atomic bomb from China, without success, and tried thereafter to build up Libya's own nuclear resources with help from Argentina, France, India, the Soviet Union, and Belgium. Even though Libya was one of the first to sign the Non-Proliferation Treaty, it has made little headway in acquiring technology and material from these outside sources: Most countries are suspicious about its intentions and provide little aid.

In 1974, Libya approached the U.S. General Atomics Corporation for assistance with nuclear technology, but nothing came of it because the State Department opposed any nuclear cooperation with Libya. The same year, Argentina agreed to train Libyan nationals to find, mine, and purify uranium (Libya had annexed a piece of Chad which has substantial uranium deposits). Whether Argentina's deal included sharing its hot cell technology with Libya is not known. Neither Argentina nor Libya had ratified the Non-Proliferation Treaty at the time, so there were no legal constraints on their exchanges.

After Libya ratified the NPT in 1975, the Soviet Union agreed to build a small research reactor, thought to have been completed in 1981. A deal with France for a nuclear power plant fell through, and in 1977 Libya agreed to buy one from the Soviet Union. Negotiations on the plant are still under way, and construction has been delayed. Whether the Soviet Union will ultimately demand return of all spent fuel from Libya, as it does with its Eastern bloc clients, is not known, but seems likely.

In 1978 Libya signed a nuclear cooperation agreement with India, but their relations ruptured when India would provide only peaceful assistance. After about a year, Libya cut off promised oil shipments to New Delhi, India recalled its ambassador, and the connection was broken.

After the Israeli raid on Iraq in 1981, Qaddafi stepped up his attempts to get nuclear technology or an actual weapon from Pakistan. He reportedly castigated President Zia for failure to deliver in return for Libya's support for the Pakistani weapons program. Qaddafi reportedly also offered Zia advanced anti-aircraft weapons to defend his nuclear plants should India attempt an Israeli-style strike against them.

In 1981 and 1982, two Belgian firms had extensive dealings with Libya, and one negotiated a deal for a uranium tetrafluoride plant. Because that substance is not itself useful in weapons production, there are no international safeguards for such facilities. However, it is easy to convert uranium tetrafluoride into uranium hexafluoride, which is used as feed material in uranium-enrichment plants. The United States successfully delayed the sale in 1984 by leaning heavily on the Belgian government, which is reconsidering the sale in light of U.S. pressure.

The Libyan-Argentine connection also grew in 1982, when Libya allegedly sent Argentina $100 million worth of weapons, including missiles, during the Falklands war. In 1983, Argentina denied that it was transferring sensitive technology to Libya. During the same period Argentina was less than forthright about its own activities, e.g., its secret enrichment plant, so the worth of its assurances may be questionable. What line the new Argentine President Raul Alfonsin may take with Libyan trade is not yet clear.

Libya poses a clear danger, and not just to Israel and the United States, its most hated enemies. After the United States downed two Libyan warplanes in the Gulf of Sidra in 1981, Qaddafi implied that he might contemplate nuclear devastation even though he lacks the bomb:

We are warning the peoples of Sicily, Crete, Turkey,

and all the states of the Mediterranean that if America again attacks the Gulf of Sidra, then we will intentionally attack the nuclear depots in their countries and cause an international catastrophe.

Qaddafi has also made inflammatory statements on the non-nuclear front, as in his speech to the Nation of Islam conference in Chicago in February of 1985, transmitted by satellite live from Libya. He called on all black American soldiers to desert their military units and form a movement to secede from the Union and establish a black American state.

Libya encapsules in a most dramatic way the dangers the world faces if proliferation is not halted. The combination of will, resources, intense hostility, and state support of terrorists could spell disaster even if the country lacks an actual bomb; if it had one, there is virtually no limit to the violence it could threaten or commit.

South Korea

Why Build the Bomb?

North and South Korea have been bitterly hostile toward each other ever since the Korean War in the early 1950s ended at an impasse, leaving the peninsula divided. The fear of invasion by the North triggered a South Korean military alert as recently as October 1983, when a group of high-ranking South Korean officials on a state visit to Burma were assassinated, allegedly by North Korean agents. There is also the fear that China could join a North Korean effort to invade the South, since China sided with and fought alongside the North Koreans during the Korean war.

The U.S. has committed thousands of American troops to the defense of South Korea. Still, during the early 1970s, South Korea began a nuclear weapons program, apparently out of fear that American commitment to its independence was beginning to waver.

Who Helped / Is Helping?

In 1972, South Korea opened secret negotiations with

France to buy a reprocessing plant. It also began buying up parts for nuclear weapons on the open market from various suppliers, including U.S. firms. The open market didn't last for long.

In the aftermath of India's 1974 test, teams of U.S. officials fanned out over the globe looking for other countries that might be in secret pursuit of the bomb. When they examined export requests at the American embassy in Seoul, everything snapped into place. Many items on South Korea's shopping list were dual purpose: They could serve industry, or they could help build the bomb.

Both the U.S. and the Suppliers Group clamped down in 1975. The U.S. pressed South Korea (which is not a UN member) into signing the Non-Proliferation Treaty by making funding for its first nuclear reactor contingent on its signature. Supplier countries agreed to restrict export of enrichment and reprocessing plants, although France argued that its prior deal with South Korea should go ahead, that it was not a proliferation risk because it was under IAEA safeguards.

The U.S. was not satisfied with this assurance, afraid that South Korea might eventually accumulate enough plutonium for nuclear weapons and then flout the safeguard system. As South Korea's main guarantor of security and source of nuclear supplies, the U.S. had a fair amount of leverage and forced South Korea to cancel its order for the French reprocessing plant in 1976.

It remains to be seen whether the U.S. will continue to have this kind of influence over South Korea in the future. If not, and if South Korean security concerns are not allayed, it would not be surprising if they resumed their efforts to obtain nuclear weapons.

Taiwan

Why Build the Bomb?

Taiwan's present security concerns are rooted in its post-World War II history: It is ruled by a minority, members of the Chinese Nationalist party who fled to the island in 1949 after losing a three-year civil war on the mainland to the Chinese Communists. Taiwan's government still claims to be the legitimate representative of all

China, while the People's Republic of China considers Taiwan part of its territory, in need of liberation from the Nationalist Chinese.

The U.S. backed the Nationalist forces during the civil war and has given them economic and military aid ever since. But the emergence of the People's Republic as a nuclear power, its displacement of Taiwan in the United Nations, and its growing diplomatic and economic ties with the United States have eroded Taiwan's position.

President Nixon's historic trip to mainland China in 1972 opened the door to developments that Taiwan could only view with alarm. Within the decade, the U.S. had granted diplomatic recognition to the People's Republic and withdrawn recognition of Taiwan, canceled its Mutual Defense Treaty with Taiwan, and withdrawn American troops from the island.

Despite continued military aid and informal security guarantees from the U.S., Taiwan is undoubtedly anxious about the intentions of its nuclear-armed neighbor and the steadfastness of American commitments in view of the U.S.-People's Republic rapprochement. The bomb may seem to the Nationalists like a weapon of last resort to prevent the People's Republic from ever reclaiming their island with impunity.

Who Helped/Is Helping?

Taiwan bought nuclear power and research reactors from the U.S. and Canada and built up a strong nuclear program in the late sixties and early seventies. It signed the Non-Proliferation Treaty in 1970, and all of its nuclear installations were brought under IAEA safeguards. During the same period, Taiwan tried to buy a reprocessing plant, first from the U.S. and then from France, without success, although France did sell some useful spare parts. In the mid-seventies, Taiwan tried to get Britain to reprocess Taiwanese spent fuel and send the plutonium back, but the U.S. blocked the deal.

Since all of its overtures had been rebuffed, Taiwan began building a small reprocessing unit on its own, having bought parts from countries all over the world, including the U.S. This Taiwanese facility was too small to produce significant amounts of plutonium and was useful mostly for training a core of Nationalist Chinese scientists. In 1975, Taiwan asked for U.S. permission to reprocess a small amount of spent fuel from a U.S.-supplied research reactor. The U.S. was uneasy about the prospect and made no reply to the request.

The next year, reports that Taiwan was secretly extracting plutonium from spent fuel at a clandestine reprocessing unit inflamed U.S. suspicions. President Ford insisted that Taiwan stop at once, dismantle the facilities and promise not to pursue any such work in the future. Taiwan had little choice but to give in to U.S. demands, since the U.S. was not only its only friend, but also its sole nuclear fuel supplier.

Like South Korea, Taiwan has for the moment been blocked on the path to nuclear weapons, but, like South Korea, it could get back on the track in fairly short order if American security guarantees seemed to be weakening. The particular danger with such isolated states is that they might soon be able to find irresponsible tutors among the new class of nuclear suppliers. States like South Africa, which is already something of an outcast in the world community, have little reason to be concerned about damaging their reputations by untoward nuclear alliances.

A 21st-Century Perspective

As you can see from the above descriptions of would-be bomb building nations, the issue of whether to try to build the bomb never goes away for technologically advanced countries--or even for those that aren't advanced. It is always on the policy options list. So far, at least seven nations (and maybe nine) have faced the option, chosen it, and succeeded. Maybe a dozen more have seriously considered the "to build or not to build" option--and passed. For now.

In the 21st century, dozens of nations will face the option on a continuing basis. How many will choose to build? That will depend mainly on how these nations evaluate their security needs: Are they better off with or without the bomb? Are their current security guarantees reliable?

Unfortunately, it will take only a relatively short period of insecurity--say, three years--for a technically developed nation to initiate and complete an irreversible nuclear weapons program. Think of it. If in all 100 years of the 21st century there is only one three-year period in which a nation (or, more precisely, its decision-makers) concludes that nuclear weapons would enhance its security and then acquires such weapons, then that nation will have a nuclear weapons capability forever. Forever.

Perhaps the greatest cause for concern is that of autocratic rulers seeking nuclear weapons as a means of maintaining their survival as heads of state. Think about how many nations have had such rulers in the 20th century--and then project the likelihood of comparable leadership taking over for the magic three-year period anytime in the rest of this century or during the next.

This kind of three-year rule (or make it a five-year rule if you want to be an optimist) points up the extraordinary challenge of halting proliferation in the absence of a fundamental change in the security environment for nation-states.

7

WHERE DO WE GO FROM HERE?

Finding a way out of the labyrinth depends on how you define the terms of this question. The last term is easy. There's not much room for argument about where we are, or, for that matter, how we got here. In the mere forty years of the Nuclear Age we have gone from zero to 50,000 nuclear weapons and from zero to at least seven, and maybe eight or nine, countries that have the bomb. Hardly a promising prospect for a planet whose sun has another five billion years of nuclear fuel.

Where we will be by the end of the next generation or two if nothing changes is a more open question, but the record of the past forty years does not inspire confidence. According to a CIA estimate, by the year 2000, fifty countries will have nuclear power plants. There will be an estimated 6,000,000 tons of fissionable material around. Any country (or technically competent group) with access to uranium can produce fissionable material on its own and, in turn, the bomb, given the will and the time. How much will and how much time are unknown factors. But also unknown is how much these estimates might change if proliferation gets the attention it warrants. We can affect the time factor somewhat with tighter technical barriers, but in the long term technical barriers can only slow a committed nation or group. If we are to *halt* proliferation, the real issue is will, a far more sobering proposition. But perhaps not hopeless.

Where we want to go in the end is harder. From the widest possible angle of vision, the desirable end is clear: If *we* means the species, the near-term destination must be "no more nuclear wars," or, more precisely, "no more nuclear weapons exploded in anger." Defining the near-term goal in this manner--versus the "nuclear disarmament" goal often cited by national leaders (most recently President Reagan and General Secretary Gorbachev)--is critically important. The track record of nuclear arms control to date makes clear that we will have to face a world in which anyone who wants the bomb

91

can get it long before the goal of nuclear disarmament is anywhere in sight.

The implications of a no-more-nuclear-wars goal are challenging and sobering. They demand attention to the fundamental question of whether nations that have nuclear weapons (or could easily build them) can fight wars with each other--and refrain from the use of nuclear weapons in the emotional ebb and flow of battle. A quick answer is to rule out big wars. Too risky. A country in a big war becomes emotional. So do its leaders. Sometimes for the good. Often not. Look at World War II.

Sober consideration of such questions quickly turns one back to the short term and the issue of how to buy enough time for political processes to work. Can a species-wide consensus on "rules of the road" for nation-state conduct in the nuclear age be developed?

Unfortunately, after forty years of the nuclear age, only one empirical "rule" emerges: No one messes much with anyone who has the bomb. In fact, if you discount the Chinese-Soviet border clashes (and the 1973 Middle East War, during which Israel probably had the bomb), you could almost refine the rule to say no one *attacks* anyone who has the bomb. Nuclear deterrence. It is not surprising in this situation that countries with security concerns choose to build nuclear weapons--and that the challenge of finding more effective ways to stem the tide of proliferation is so great.

What about the short term? Immediately. What can be done now? What can we do more of? What new can be done? Are there new processes to try?

In the material that follows, we have addressed these questions with a structure based on a question process. Where can we go to work and with whom? What in the near term are the alternative forums for additional effort? In addition, since halting proliferation turns on action over time--which correlates with the number of actors that have to strike a deal--in this chapter we will move from smaller to gradually larger circles of nation actors. We will consider what ever-larger combinations of nations might do--presuming one of the nations is always the United States. In the last section we will try to assess what might be possible in the near term-- what we, as citizens and human beings, might hope to accomplish in our time.

You might wonder why we are using "nation" as the unit capable of acting. When empires died and "all the great words were cancelled out" during World War I, "nation" was one word that arose from their demise. It gained even more ground after World War II. There are 169 nations, at last count. We have seen the deleterious impact on past non-proliferation efforts of a few nation-states not agreeing to proposed rules. It makes you realize that the set of rules it will take to halt proliferation must be adopted by nearly all nations. A few outlaws might be barely tolerable--but only a few. It's a tough order, which by its very nature demands a long view--and a focus on nations. Consider them. The number will not change much in the period--two, maybe three generations at the outside--that we have to work this problem. And neither will their characters. For better or worse, these are the nations that are the actors in the attempt to control proliferation. The children alive today in all of them will know the outcome.

We'll begin with the nation the authors of this book know best--the United States. The first instinct of Americans is to ask what the United States can do alone. It's inherent in its citizens' self-reliance and their view of government and rules. The United States would like to be able to halt proliferation by itself. It can't. But there is a menu of things to do and things to do better. Likewise with the other groups of nations. You should be aware, before plunging in, that the menu that follows is just that--and not a prescription. Experts might call it a policy options menu. The intent is to reexamine the awesome problem of halting proliferation in a coherent and systematic manner. We do not claim to know the right answers--the choices to make--but we do believe we have posed the right questions.

Forum No. 1: The United States

Enact a New U.S. Non-Proliferation Act?

The United States already has one of the most stringent sets of laws controlling the export of nuclear materials and equipment, mandated by the 1978 Nuclear Non-Proliferation Act. However, there is enough ambiguity in that act to allow decisions that clearly contravene its intent, even if they do not violate the actual letter of the law. A recent example is the 1984 executive-branch decision to permit the export of U.S. nuclear power reactors to China in the absence of any written agreements as to what follow-on projects the Chinese contemplate with the technology and materials they receive (although an agreement on the subsequent use of plutonium of U.S. origin may yet emerge).

If there is to be a law of the land on proliferation, then it must be unambiguous and consistently enforced, particularly if we hope to hold ourselves up as an example to other nuclear supplier nations. A new and tougher Nuclear Non-Proliferation Act may be useful to this end. It might also provide a good opportunity for the Congress to debate in depth the long-term implications of U.S. nuclear export policy.

Constrain Foreign Subsidiaries of U.S. Companies?

Under present law, U.S. companies frequently license their foreign subsidiaries to produce and sell nuclear equipment and materials. While the U.S. firms retain rights to approve subsequent resale of such technology, this has become a gray area for enforcement, especially after the Soviet gas pipeline controversy in which the U.S. tried to enforce similar restrictions and failed. As a consequence, foreign subsidiaries have something of a free hand in marketing U.S. nuclear technology, a special concern in light of the 1980 Non-Proliferation Act restrictions on countries that do not accept full-scope safeguards. Thus, a follow-on to any new and more restrictive Non-Proliferation Act might bring U.S. subsidiaries under the same constraints that apply to their parent companies.

Offer Security Guarantees to More Nations?

Today the United States offers by treaty a security guarantee, virtually a nuclear pact, to the following nations:

NATO Treaty (1947): Belgium, Denmark, Britain, Greece, Italy, Luxemburg, The Netherlands, Norway, Portugal, Spain, West Germany, Iceland, Turkey, France (planning only).

U.S.-Japan Treaty (1948): Japan.

ANZUS Treaty (1951): Australia and New Zealand

While these treaties remain intact, there is growing concern that formal U.S. security guarantees are of less utility than was once the case. For example, in February 1985, New Zealand refused to allow U.S. ships to call at its ports because the U.S. would not say whether the ships were armed with nuclear weapons--which is standard U.S. practice at ports around the world. According to Secretary of State George Shultz, "New Zealand has basically taken a walk" from the alliance. State Department officials say that the U.S. will continue selling some arms to New Zealand but will no longer treat it as an ally. Australia is still in; it doesn't make the same demands on U.S. warships.

The U.S. has also made strong security commitments, as evidenced by military aid, to nations like Israel, Egypt, Pakistan, South Korea, and Taiwan.

Would more such guarantees help curb nuclear proliferation? Britain and France chose nuclear weapons in spite of the ironclad guarantees of the NATO treaty--an attack against one is an attack against all. And Israel apparently did not have enough faith in the security guarantees implicit in the significant military aid the U.S. provided to forego the nuclear option. Neither did South Korea or Taiwan at the time they began nuclear weapons programs.

Still, there might be some nations that would decide against building nuclear weapons, at least temporarily, if the U.S. guaranteed their security. It is the temporal nature of such commitments that makes them of dubious value over the long haul. At no time can there be a period of a few years during which such countries view the U.S. commitment as shaky, or the "to build or not to build" decision will come up again, perhaps to be reversed and implemented.

The security-guarantee route to halting nuclear proliferation is also limited by the fact that the U.S. is unlikely to offer such promises to many of the nations on the brink of developing nuclear weapons, such as South Africa and Argentina. Even in the case of Taiwan, U.S. security commitments may appear less credible as the U.S.-China relationship matures.

Withhold Economic and Military Aid?

The withdrawal of economic and military aid offers another means of control over would-be proliferators. To date, this type of leverage had been used selectively.

In the case of the nascent South Korean and Taiwanese nuclear programs, the threat of withdrawal of military aid was an important factor in dissuading these nations from proceeding with their atomic plans. U.S. law resulted in the use of this kind of leverage with Pakistan for a short time, but the U.S. continues to see its short-term interest in helping the Afghan rebels via bases in Pakistan as more important to U.S. security. The story with Israel is less clear. There is no evidence that the U.S. government has ever threatened to withdraw or withhold aid to Israel to get that nation to sign the Non-Proliferation Treaty or accept full-scope IAEA safeguards. Yet Israel receives the largest military aid package of any U.S. ally.

In terms of direct economic aid, the sums involved are modest, and there has been little effort to tie such aid to nation-state behavior on the proliferation issue.

Ban the Export of Reactors?

Banning the export of nuclear reactors for power or research would be an extraordinary measure for the United States to take. It would mean reversing the Atoms for Peace commitment to aggressive promotion of reactor exports. It would also be a violation of those sections of the Non-Proliferation Treaty that guarantee nuclear power to nations that agree to accept IAEA safeguards and not to build nuclear weapons. Nevertheless, getting a reactor is a giant step toward getting the bomb, and we might want to consider such a ban and then promote this approach to other reactor-exporting nations.

Forum No. 2: The U.S. and the U.S.S.R.

No two nations have a greater stake in halting nuclear proliferation--or more leverage to do so--than the two superpowers, yet their efforts to resolve the problem in concert have been modest at best. While the superpowers' joint efforts were critical to the establishment of the IAEA, the Non-Proliferation Treaty, and the Suppliers Group, they have been unable to solve problems such as the Chinese and French rejection of the NPT and the more critical individual nation problems that have emerged (India, Israel, Pakistan, etc.). The problem, of course, is the abysmal state of relations between the two nations--and especially their preoccupation with negotiations to limit their respective long-range nuclear arsenals.

If the superpowers could commit far greater time and energy to the proliferation issue--in effect forge a strong working relationship--the potential for resolving the problem would be substantial, considering that the driving force for proliferation is nation-state security, something the two big kids on the block can affect considerably. Simply put, joint initiatives on security issues by the owners of over ninety-five percent of the world's nuclear weapons is bound to carry significant weight. How to get them started is the problem.

Limit Superpower Arsenals?

Under Article VI of the Non-Proliferation Treaty, the "have" nations agree to constrain their arsenals as part of the bargain struck with "have-not" nations that agree not to build nuclear weapons. While there has been some progress on arms control, the superpowers' nuclear arsenals stand at about 25,000 warheads apiece, with roughly ten thousand apiece in their strategic forces (long-range bombers and missiles). The other major nuclear powers--Britain, France, and China--will soon have roughly two thousand nuclear weapons among them and yet have never been involved in a single negotiation on limiting their arsenals.

The potential impact on "have-not" nations of a superpower nuclear-arms reduction rarely surfaces in deliberations on strategy or tactics for superpower nuclear-arms control. But obviously it should be driving force. A real U.S.-Soviet effort to control their military competition *and* reduce the growth in their nuclear arsenals could be a profoundly positive signal to countries on the threshold of nuclear acquisition. It would at least undercut the argument that the nuclear powers, and especially the United States and the Soviet Union, are violating the spirit and the letter of Article VI of the Non-Proliferation Treaty.

Fortunately, the superpowers are continuing their efforts to negotiate limits on their nuclear arsenals. There is little question that both sides share the goal of halting their nuclear competition. However, the differences in force structures on the two sides have made these negotiations protracted and contentious. Begun in 1969, arms negotiations have yet to effect an in-force agreement on offensive nuclear weapons.

Clearly it is imperative that the two superpowers get past this formidable road block--and not just to comply with Article VI of the NPT. Of even greater significance is the need for the top leadership in the two countries to devote more time to proliferation--and to the world hot spots which brew interest in the bomb to meet security concerns.

Joint Security Guarantees?

Imagine a schoolyard wherein two kids from different sides of the tracks are much bigger than anybody else and offer to protect the little kids. Will the U.S. and the Soviet Union ever be able to play this role in the world?

Perhaps in time, but not soon. The two superpowers are nowhere near developing a civil relationship, much less a working relationship or a security-motivated partnership that other nations could count on to last. Nations would have to trust in the U.S. and the Soviet Union and in their lasting partnership before they could tie their security to the concerted actions of the two superpowers. It is hard to imagine getting to that state before another generation or two has passed. Nevertheless, there might be regions, say, the Middle East or the Persian Gulf, where joint superpower security guarantees would be useful in the coming decades.

Joint U.S.-Soviet Use of Force?

If the U.S. and the Soviet Union agreed that a nation that is pursuing the bomb should not have such weapons, they could conceivably undertake joint military action to destroy that nation's nuclear facilities. Such action would presumably be taken only as a last resort, after all possible diplomatic and economic sanctions had been exhausted.

Would such a U.S.-Soviet nuclear SWAT team be politically and militarily feasible? For starters, this approach would require a viable U.S.-Soviet relationship--no mean task. In addition, it would require case-by-case agreement on which country's nuclear programs should be abruptly halted (a complexity the Israelis did not have to face when they bombed the Iraqi nuclear facility). This is the real problem with this approach.

Getting superpower agreement on who should and who should not pursue nuclear weapons is a tough order. Consider, for example, the four countries that we characterized earlier as de facto Nuclear Club members: India, Israel, Pakistan, and South Africa. Needless to say, it is virtually inconceivable that the U.S. and the Soviet Union could agree to take out the nuclear facilities in any of these countries. Even with rogue nations--take Libya and Iran, for example--there is no reason to hope that the superpowers could achieve consensus on whether such nations should be attacked. At some future time, joint U.S.-Soviet action against terrorists with the bomb might prove practical, but direct superpower attacks on nation-states are unlikely to prove an effective non-proliferation measure.

Forum No. 3: The Nuclear Club

In the thirty-five years that the Nuclear Club has existed there has never been a meeting of its members to discuss their special status--and the problem of controlling nuclear weapons. Unbelievable, but true. Why? If you ask an international relations expert, you will get a long lecture on Nuclear Age politics, which is likely to leave you shaking your head and asking "But why not now?" It's a good question. The Nuclear Clubhouse would seem to be a good place to hold a meeting to discuss both rules for members and what to do about would-be members.

There is, however, one modest example of cooperation among Club members. If you have crashed into the Club and want to know how to make bombs that are safe to transport and store (through fancy codes and mechanisms that ensure that they don't go off by accident), the Club will help you out. A nation that has just had its first successful nuclear weapons test would undoubtedly get a positive response to a letter sent to the national capitals of Club members, asking for such information. Maybe even some blueprints left on their doorsteps one night. And for good reason. A fully loaded U.S. B-52 accidentally lost a couple of twenty-four megaton bombs over a farm in Goldsboro, North Carolina, in 1961. Several locks on one of the bombs had been triggered and depending on whose story you believe, only one or two remaining switches prevented the bomb from detonating. These devices also make it extremely difficult, if not impossible, to explode a stolen bomb. Once you're in the Club, nobody wants any accidents.

Ban on Nuclear Weapons Testing?

Today three Nuclear Club members--the United States, the Soviet Union, and Britain--have signed the 1963 Limited Test Ban Treaty prohibiting nuclear weapons tests in space, in the atmosphere, and underwater, but not underground. These same nations have also had on-again, off-again negotiations on a ban on all nuclear weapons testing--called a Comprehensive Test Ban. However, to date, France and China have rejected all entreaties to join in such negotiations, although France now conducts its tests underground in the South Pacific.

A complete halt to *all* nuclear weapons testing would send a clear signal that Nuclear Club members are genuinely serious about halting the nuclear arms race, at least in terms of further modernization of nuclear weapons. This would help to encourage would-be Club members to hold off from proceeding with a nuclear weapons program, but probably only if the test ban applied to all nuclear weapons states. Such a comprehensive treaty would be extremely difficult to achieve without a fundamental change in attitude by France and China.

Another problem is the skepticism with which a comprehensive test ban is regarded in parts of the national security community in both the United States and the Soviet Union. The military is dubious as to whether the costs outweigh the benefits.

In the U.S. the prospect of using nuclear weapons to power space-based lasers in the "Star Wars" program, and the need for an extensive testing program in this context, is also an impediment to a comprehensive ban. There are also serious disagreements about the problem of verifying such a ban, although substantial progress, to include in-country monitoring devices, was made on this front before the U.S./Soviet/British negotiations ended in 1980.

Enact a Global Ceiling on Nuclear Weapons?

The recent discovery of the "nuclear winter" effect of detonating a small fraction of the world arsenal--cold and darkness over much of the earth produced by smoke particles in the upper atmosphere blocking out sunlight-- must, in time, dramatically alter our thinking about even "limited" nuclear wars. But we have not even begun to wrestle with the implications of nuclear winter--such as whether any one nation on the planet, much less one person, should even have the option of launching a nu- clear winter inducing attack.

Although the nuclear winter calculations are still being refined, the predicted damage to the climate of even a "small" exchange of a hundred weapons is sobering enough to suggest that the existing nuclear powers not run the experiment--and that we take action on the proli- feration front to ensure that some future India-Pakistan or Argentina-Brazil war does not do so either. Why challenge our species and all others to survive a new Ice Age, when the dinosaurs and most other species alive at the time didn't survive the last one?

This potentially catastrophic impact of a nuclear war could motivate Nuclear Club members to reduce their com- bined nuclear arsenals to levels that ensure that if a nuclear war should occur, it would not threaten the survival of the human species. But with an arsenal of 50,000 weapons and counting, it would be naive for the Club to set very ambitious near-term reduction goals. A ceiling at or near current levels might do for starters. A transition to some reduction goal might follow. How- ever, even if there is significant progress in arms control, it is hard to see how the world's arsenal could get below, say, even the 5,000-weapon level for another generation or two at best.

Forum No. 4: Nuclear Supplier Nations

The nuclear equipment supplier nations are currently the most active forum for fighting nuclear proliferation. This results from their recognition that India, Israel, Pakistan, South Africa, Argentina, Taiwan, and other states have advanced toward the nuclear threshold as a consequence of insufficient restraint on the part of international suppliers over a period of almost thirty years. A far higher level of cooperation among supplier nations could help to block this route to Club membership. However, it should be emphasized that many of the nations of most concern to non-proliferation efforts (e.g., India, Israel, Pakistan, South Africa, Argentina, Brazil) are already beyond dependence on outside suppliers and may, in fact, be interested in entering the nuclear-supply market themselves.

Adopt U.S. Non-Proliferation Act Constraints?

If rigid export rules akin to those of the U.S. Non-Proliferation Act were adopted by all supplier nations, it would be a major step toward curbing proliferation. Getting agreement to more restrictive export rules has been the U.S. goal in ongoing discussions among supplier nations from both superpower camps. The most problematic nations in these negotiations are some of the U.S.'s Western European allies, notably France and Germany, and neutral Switzerland. In fact, the Swiss government makes the astonishing claim that it has little control over the nuclear equipment exporting practices of its engineering firms.

A near-term focus on constraining supplier nations clearly makes sense, since slowing proliferation in the near term is critical to buying the time needed to halt proliferation in the long term. Still, many of the horses are out of the barn: Nearly thirty nations already have nuclear power reactors, although most today are under at least some safeguards.

Insist on Return of Spent Fuel?

At present, the Soviet Union is the only supplier nation that normally demands eventual return of all exported fuel rods (although it has not yet insisted on this with Cuba). An agreement among supplier nations insisting that all spent fuel be sent back to its country of origin would be a major step in reducing the threat of covert reprocessing. (But again it should be kept in mind that countries such as Pakistan, South Africa, Argentina, et al., are following the uranium-enrichment route to obtain at least some of their fissionable material.)

Ban on Reprocessing of Spent Fuel?

There are enough confirmed uranium deposits in the world to fuel all conceivable nuclear reactors for the foreseeable future. Thus, spent fuel need not be reprocessed to meet the demands for fissionable material, unless a country (France is an example) has invested major resources in plutonium-fueled reactors for nuclear power. If the supplier nations could agree to a global ban on reprocessing and the burning up of existing plutonium in existing reactors, they could effect a rapid reduction in the amount of plutonium in circulation. But unanimity would be imperative.

Ban the Export of All Reactors?

In light of the danger of proliferation that is present once a nation gets a nuclear reactor, a complete ban on the export of nuclear reactors might be considered. However, access to nuclear power by some nations but not others would not be feasible as a long-term global policy without other changes. For example, for such a ban to be palatable, there would, as a minimum, have to be a corollary effort to develop alternative power sources for countries that had planned to import reactors for their energy needs, as well as some mechanism for sharing research reactor facilities.

Forum No. 5: The Uranium Supplier Nations

As the technology for uranium enrichment becomes more widely available, the uranium supplier nations might offer a particularly useful forum for seeking constraints on possession and distribution of uranium. As noted below, for this forum to erect barriers would prove especially difficult given the nature of the trade and the countries involved in it.

Enact Uranium Export Restrictions?

The uranium-mining countries (see Appendix D) are a disparate group of developed and developing nations. And, to date, there has been no attempt among them to control export of raw uranium ore or processed uranium (so-called yellowcake). If these countries could agree on export guidelines, the flow of uranium ore that might, in turn, be used to produce weapons-grade enriched uranium could be constrained.

One near-term approach might be to ban exports of uranium to:

(1) Countries that have not signed the Non-Proliferation Treaty;

(2) Countries that export nuclear materials and equipment to countries that have not signed the Non-Proliferation Treaty;

(3) Nuclear Club members that have not signed the Limited Test Ban Treaty or some future comprehensive test ban treaty.

Keep in mind, however, that these restrictions would not affect most of the nations of near-term concern, because they already have substantial uranium supplies. For example, South Africa extracts uranium from gold-mining residues, and Israel gets it from phosphate deposits, etc.

As with the export of nuclear equipment and materials, the economic impact of curtailing uranium exports must be recognized. Many of the uranium-exporting nations are economically dependent on the income from uranium exports. In fact, it would undoubtedly prove very difficult to reach agreements restricting uranium exports, except in the context of a global effort to halt proliferation-related exports, that is, after exerting more comprehensive and ambitious efforts than anything seen to date.

Halt All Uranium Mining?

A global halt to uranium mining, say, by the year 2000 or not long thereafter, would signal a shift away from nuclear power--and the threat of proliferation inherent in it.

Uranium mining countries would find such a ban to be a serious economic burden, especially developing countries like Niger, the world's fifth-largest exporter of uranium ore. Perhaps members of the international community benefiting security-wise from the prohibition would have to share the cost of this lost trade in some manner. The alternative, an almost unlimited amount of uranium in circulation around the world, presents an extraordinary challenge to presumable 21st- and 22nd-century efforts to hold back proliferation.

Could the planet eventually turn its back on uranium--use up what we have taken from the ground, close up the existing mines, and be assured that no uranium were ever mined again? The challenge to verification is severe. There is a lot of uranium in places other than where commercial mining currently takes place. Whether future technology could provide adequate monitoring devices for a ban (fortunately, it's all radioactive, which is how people find it in the first place) is a matter of debate. Obviously, an extraordinary degree of international cooperation would be required, involving essentially all nations.

Forum No. 6: The International Community

One of the most poignant lessons learned from non-proliferation efforts to date is the need for unanimous actions among all nations if any long-term non-proliferation strategy is to work. This is painfully evident in the failure to gain universal acceptance of the Non-Proliferation Treaty. Because two nuclear states (China and France) and many other potential nuclear weapons states (India, Israel, Pakistan, South Africa, Brazil, and Argentina) have refused to sign the NPT, it has not been the effective instrument that its creators envisioned. In fact, the formal Treaty Review Conferences (at five-year intervals starting in 1975) have to date been little more than forums in which the non-nuclear weapons states berate the three sheepish Nuclear Club signatories for their failure to live up to the Article VI commitment to negotiate limits on their nuclear arsenals. Based on this experience, what are the agreements--the nuclear rules of the road for planet Earth--that might, in time, be negotiated among *all* the nations of the world?

Promote Global Approval of The Non-Proliferation Treaty?

Continued pursuit of global endorsement of the Non-Proliferation Treaty is useful, even if there are no improvements in the existing treaty and even if the number of nuclear weapons states eventually grows to ten or more nations. If the effort is to succeed, fence-sitting nations such as India, Israel, and South Africa will have to choose whether they will follow the NPT rules for have or for have-not nations. Aggressive pursuit of France and China on the NPT issue would also serve to clarify whether these nations see any broader global responsibility (or desire) to halt the spread of nuclear weapons.

Negotiate a New Non-Proliferation Treaty: NPT II?

Just as the SALT I Interim Agreement limiting super-power strategic offensive nuclear weapons (long-range bombers and missiles) was followed by a far more comprehensive SALT II Treaty, so might the existing Non-Proliferation Treaty be followed by a more restrictive NPT II. NPT II could make provisions to close the loopholes of NPT I and the associated UN-monitored IAEA safeguards system. Possible changes could include a much longer escape clause, a strong and numerically explicit commitment to reducing existing arsenals by Club members (e.g., a few percent a year), a no-warning inspection system for the IAEA, and sanctions for violations by treaty signatories.

The danger here is that if a new NPT conference failed dramatically, it could undermine the existing treaty entirely or yield a follow-on treaty even less effective than the present one. This dangerous prospect has made many experts cautious about pursuing new treaty negotiations at this time.

International Control of All Spent Fuel?

An international spent fuel dump would significantly reduce the risk of covert reprocessing of such fuel to recover plutonium. It might also set the stage for eventual international cooperation to dispose of this and other radioactive waste in some futuristic dump, say, deep in the earth's mantel or in a disposable spaceship aimed toward the ultimate dump, the sun. An initiative of this kind is fairly daunting: The problem of getting all nations to sign is dwarfed by the problem of getting any nation to agree to accept the safety burden of huge quantities of spent fuel and other waste.

Future Global Ban on Nuclear Reactors?

Because nuclear reactors are a principal source of proliferation concern, a global goal of getting out of the nuclear power business as soon as possible might be examined. With such a goal, international efforts to develop safer power sources would be pursued with far more energy. At the same time it must be recognized that the absence of nuclear reactors would only stem the plutonium route to nuclear proliferation. The increasingly popular, and much harder to constrain, enriched-uranium route would still remain.

Other Forums: Space

If you have concluded at this point that the policy options for pursuing non-proliferation goals on planet Earth are pretty thin gruel, you're right. With this rationale--and with an eye to a little relief--it may be excusable to look beyond earthly solutions, just to see more clearly what a dire predicament we may be in.

If reduction of the global arsenal to safe (i.e., below nuclear winter) levels is impossible in the next century or so, it may make sense for the human species to hedge against the fate of the earth through a global effort at space colonization. We might possibly strike out for another planet or moon in this solar system or, in time, a habitable planet in some nearby star system. Unfortunately, the closest star is several light years away, far beyond the reach of any space travel technology likely to emerge in the next generation or two.

On the other hand, there is a possibility that other intelligent life in our own Milky Way galaxy has survived the Nuclear Age--in which case, we might consider sending a "How did you do it?" query to the 200,000,000,000 stars in our galaxy. For example, we might concentrate on those stars for which we are now finding evidence of planetary systems.

If there is intelligent life in our galaxy that has survived the struggle of Nuclear Age adolescence--perhaps we could get some cosmic "do's and don'ts" from them before we queer the deal on this planet. But how long would it take for even an advanced civilization to understand our predicament and figure out how to help? A message to even the closest star would take six years to send out and return--and most of the stars in our Milky Way are thousands of light years away. So help might be a long time coming, if it's out there at all.

That leaves us back on planet Earth, and on our own. But ours is a species that has shown remarkable staying power over the years. And it's not as though we can't think of anything to do about the problem. We can--as the menu in this chapter clearly reveals. But can we do enough, fast enough? And where should we start? And who should do it?

Next Steps

In this book "Where do we go from here?" is a question for Americans. Where does the United States of America go from here? And since this is one of those issues for which there is no effective alternative to acting through government, where do the people of the United States want the government of the United States to go from here?

First and foremost, it is clear that the government *and* the people of the United States need to spend a lot more time on this issue--and right now. This problem needs work.

As a citizen, there is one short-term mission that you can undertake on your own and that is educating other people, in your family, your classroom, your workplace, your neighborhood, or your place of worship, on this subject. You might even want to find out what your local public utility company knows about proliferation, or your local government. A major reason for the failure so far to deal effectively with proliferation is that there are just too few people who see the immediacy of the problem. Only a general awareness of the problem can create the kind of groundswell needed to move it high enough up the list of priorities, for the U.S. government and for other governments around the world.

In the long term, we must recognize that it is the entire species that must find a solution to this complex problem. Getting there will demand a level of good will and thought and cooperation never before seen on a global scale, a shared purpose so powerful that it transcends all international animosity. It is the only way to avoid the almost certain destruction of civilization itself.

It is only this shared goal that can make possible a new set of Rules of the Nuclear Road to which all nation-states will subscribe. And it must be *all* nations: Anything short of unanimity is tantamount to a perfidious distraction--and potentially worse than no rules at all-- because it will waste precious time. Most of the rules that can be imagined will require nations to yield some small element of their national sovereignty and independence to the common good. Not world government, by any means, but world appreciation of our shared fate and recognition that we must either cooperate or self-destruct. That should not be too high a price to pay for averting a holocaust.

Building a worldwide edifice that works on top of the existing rough framework, with its limited success in dealing with proliferation, is a tall order. But we can bring it off if we are a species with a will to survive. If we succeed, we will have earned the label *sapiens*. We will be a species that is in some cosmic sense worth-while.

As we examine the means of bringing new vigor and commitment to the proliferation problem, it is increasingly clear that the few promising alternatives that do exist either: (1) involve joint U.S.-Soviet action, e.g., progress on superpower nuclear arms control, or (2) require a joint (and strong) U.S.-Soviet effort within a broader group of nation-states (especially within the Nuclear Club or within the international community as a whole). This should not be surprising since it is the super power of their nuclear arsenals that gives these two nations their joint sobriquet. But how can the better working relationship that non-proliferation demands be effected? And how can it be done quickly?

Obviously, the first step for the two nations is to get past their preoccupation with their own nuclear competition. In over fifteen years of negotiating on those weapons, there is to date only one agreement, the Anti-Ballistic Missile Treaty, limiting defensive weapons. Two agreements limiting offensive weapons to roughly current levels have been reached, but neither is in effect (although both nations appear to be adhering to the unratified SALT II Treaty). If we go through another fifteen years of such negotiations with no more progress than this, we can kiss all long-term non-proliferation efforts good-bye. Otherwise we will adopt the same posture as a chain-smoker who puffs away while trying to persuade others that smoking is bad for their health.

But if we can halt and then *reverse* the U.S.-Soviet nuclear competition--and render it a subject pursued mainly by experts along clear guidelines--then the considerable energy and power of the United States and the Soviet Union can be brought to bear on the proliferation problem.

The first obstacle after that presented by superpower competition is obviously the one posed by the other nuclear powers. If France, China, and Britain are not also committed to halting proliferation as a national objective, then we can also forget it, and spend our energies trying to figure out how to survive on a planet where the bomb is a common possession.

Finally, the U.S. and the Soviet Union, accompanied by the other major powers, must find a way to satisfy the security concerns of both the de facto Nuclear Club members and the other near-nuclear nations described in this book. If this next batch of maybe/maybe not Club members forces its way in the door, we can probably forget it as well.

The precise kinds of "deals" that these nations should make--about security or weapons--remain to be seen. But the most troubling concern of all is that right now, in the face of the scant progress to date and the low priority given the issue, it would not be an exaggeration to claim that we as humans are simply not working the problem.

8

HOW TO MAKE A DIFFERENCE

Unfortunately, it will appear
to many people premature to
take some action until it will
be too late to take any
action.

--Leo Szilard, 1939

Leo Szilard was talking about action on a different sort of proliferation--the spread of the new physics across national borders of countries that were soon to be at war with each other. It took him five years to get physicists to see that they should not be so free with their papers. Had it taken longer, the outcome of World War II could have been vastly different.

Although we've taken Szilard's statement out of context, it works as well in the context of the new, immediate danger proliferation presents. Time is of the essence if any of the options presented in the last chapter are to be brought into being before the world changes beyond recognition.

Policy Roadmap: Places Where You Can Have an Impact

In order to act effectively, you need to understand how decisions on U.S. non-proliferation policy are made. When the U.S. policy-making process is working properly, the Congress and the president share the power to make policy. However, in the area of proliferation, as in almost all other areas with a strong international-relations component, far and away the greatest power and influence rest in the executive branch. The Founding Fathers in the United States virtually guaranteed this situation by investing the president with "executive power" for the nation and especially the power to make treaties, appoint ambassadors, etc., albeit with the consent of Congress. Despite efforts by the Congress to gain more of a foothold in foreign affairs, this arena

Nuclear Non-Proliferation Policy Road Map

TESTIMONY BY EXECUTIVE BRANCH OFFICIALS AND OTHERS

TESTIMONY BY EXECUTIVE BRANCH OFFICIALS AND OTHERS

TESTIMONY BY EXECUTIVE BRANCH OFFICIALS AND OTHERS

TESTIMONY BY EXECUTIVE BRANCH OFFICIALS AND OTHERS

TESTIMONY BY EXECUTIVE BRANCH OFFICIALS AND OTHERS

FOREIGN RELATIONS COMMITTEE

ENERGY COMMITTEE

GOVERNMENT AFFAIRS COMMITTEE

FOREIGN AFFAIRS COMMITTEE

ENERGY & COMMERCE COMMITTEE

SENATE / HOUSE

LEGISLATION

LEGISLATION

SOME POLICY PROPOSALS

PRESIDENT

POLICY OPTIONS PAPER

POLICY PROPOSALS

OTHER NATIONS

SPECIAL INTERAGENCY GROUP

POLICY OPTIONS AND ARGUMENTS

STATE
Secretary of State
- Ambassador for Non-Proliferation
- Asst. Sec'y for Oceans, Environment and Int'l Scientific Affairs

ENERGY
Secretary of Energy
- Asst. Sec'y for Defense Programs
- Asst. Sec'y for Int'l Affairs

DEFENSE
Secretary of Defense
- Asst. Sec'y for Int'l Security Affairs

ARMS CONTROL AND DISARMAMENT AGENCY (ACDA)
Director of ACDA
- Asst. Director for Nuclear Weapons and Control

NUCLEAR REGULATORY COMMISSION (NRC)
NRC Chairman & Commissioners
- Office of International Programs

COMMERCE
Secretary of Commerce
- Asst. Sec'y for Int'l Commerce

Artwork, Michelle Higgins

remains the stronghold of the president. Nuclear proliferation is no exception.

In the proliferation area, however, Congress has demonstrated a will and an ability to influence policy. Although we have come to a state of affairs in U.S. nuclear proliferation policy where almost all of the interesting policy options involve deliberations and negotiations with other states--the clear province of the executive branch--Congress can and does play an important role in proliferation policy--for example, voting to withhold economic or military aid to a would-be proliferator. Nonetheless, in terms of new policy initiatives, the Congress is basically in a reactive (versus an active) mode, i.e., it can pass judgment on executive branch initiatives, but cannot undertake significant new initiatives itself.

The only president in the Nuclear Age with any technical background was Jimmy Carter, who had attended the Navy's nuclear submarine officer-training program. This at least gave him the ability to speak the technical language of nuclear power and nuclear weapons, but, like all other presidents, he was heavily dependent on executive branch experts in the various departments (State, Defense, Energy, etc.) for the formulation and evaluation of new nuclear-proliferation policy initiatives.

The congressional bodies responsible for nuclear proliferation issues are the Foreign Affairs Committee in the House and the Foreign Relations, Governmental Affairs, and Energy and National Resources Committees in the Senate. The most important examples of congressional legislation affecting non-proliferation policy have been the 1954 Atomic Energy Act and the 1978 Nuclear Non-Proliferation Act. However, these laws are carried out by executive departments and agencies, and since there is often ambiguity in the laws--and therefore wide latitude in how they are interpreted--the policy statements issued by the executive branch can have nearly as much impact as the laws do.

A good example of this ambiguity in enforcement of non-proliferation laws concerns the question of whether plutonium should be extracted from spent fuel for reuse as fuel itself in breeder reactors. Presidents Ford, Carter, and Reagan used their discretionary power of interpretation to put forth quite different policies on this question, during a period when the laws in force remained essentially the same. In 1976, President Ford reversed the trend of earlier policy by saying that the U.S. should not favor the use of plutonium at all. The next year, President Carter took the additional step of saying that the U.S. would actively try to discourage plutonium use throughout the world. In 1981, President Reagan said his administration would encourage use of plutonium in this country and not try to discourage it in Western Europe or Japan, but would follow the Carter policy in countries that looked like would-be proliferators.

Because of the power of the president over proliferation matters, a who's who of executive branch policy-making bodies is in order here so that you will recognize key players in the policy-making process. See the chart later in this chapter for a schematic view of the inter-relationships among these bodies within the executive branch and between the executive branch and the Congress.

Department of State

To date, the Department of State has been the lead executive agency concerned with nuclear proliferation issues, although the Arms Control and Disarmament Agency has also had a significant impact on policy in this area. In the Reagan administration, the main actors at State are the ambassador-at-large for nuclear non-proliferation and the assistant secretary for oceans, environment, and international scientific affairs. The State Department is not only the main source of nuclear proliferation policy initiatives, but the main enforcer and negotiator as well. It negotiates with foreign governments, gathers agency and departmental views on export licenses for the Nuclear Regulatory Commission, and represents the United States at the IAEA. Together with the Department of Energy, the State Department decides whether U.S. nuclear technology can be transferred from one country to another and whether countries that have imported U.S. fuel will be allowed to reprocess it to extract plutonium. Interagency deliberations on new nuclear proliferation policy initiatives generally take place within a Special Interagency Group which then forwards policy options to the president for decision.

Department of Energy

The main actors at the Department of Energy are the assistant secretary for defense programs and the assistant secretary for international affairs. DOE has the major voice in the joint decision with State about technology transfer and plutonium reprocessing. It does research on nuclear power and makes decisions about managing nuclear waste. It also is responsible for building and testing all U.S. nuclear warheads and produces all U.S. nuclear weapons material, by far the largest line item in its budget.

Arms Control and Disarmament Agency

The main actor at ACDA is the assistant director for nuclear weapons and control. ACDA's exclusive responsibility is arms control matters; in effect, it prods the executive branch to consider arms control approaches aimed at enhancing U.S. security. It advises on all nuclear proliferation policy decisions and prepares formal statements for the Congress (called Arms Control Impact Statements) on the most critical of those decisions. It also houses the administration's resident experts on IAEA safeguards.

Nuclear Regulatory Commission

The main actors at NRC are the five commissioners, one of whom is chairman. The NRC issues export licenses for nuclear fuel, reactors, and components. After the NRC gets a request for an export license, it passes the request on to the State Department. The State Department gathers the opinions of all interested agencies and departments and sends them back to the NRC. Applying standards set forth in law, the NRC then rules on the request. The president can overrule the NRC if it denies a license that the State Department approves, but then Congress reviews the president's decision. The NRC is also responsible for regulating safety standards at nuclear power and nuclear waste management programs. It offers advice on all other non-proliferation policy decisions. Unlike the other agencies under discussion, the NRC is "independent," that is, the president cannot fire its commissioners because he doesn't like their decisions. They serve five-year terms and can be removed only for gross incompetence.

Commerce Department

The main actor at Commerce is the assistant secretary for international trade. Commerce issues licenses for "dual use" items, such as large computers that can be used either for nuclear or industrial purposes. Generally, the Departments of State and Energy and the Arms Control and Disarmament Agency have a say in these decisions. Commerce also gives advice on all other nuclear non-proliferation decisions involving export items.

Department of Defense

The main actor at the Department of Defense is the assistant secretary for international security affairs. The Department of Defense participates in interagency meetings on nuclear non-proliferation policy decisions. Although it has traditionally maintained a low profile in this area, this situation is changing in the direction of more active involvement in these decisions. DoD often plays a major role in non-proliferation decision making when nuclear issues have a direct impact on U.S. security assistance to another country.

Congressional Testimony

Executive branch agencies are called on from time to time to testify before congressional committees having an interest in nuclear proliferation policy. The State Department is usually the agency that testifies.

A good case study in non-proliferation policy-making where there was a strong disagreement between the administration and the Congress is the 1982-83 exercise whereby the administration attempted to adopt more liberal export policies with respect to certain potential proliferators. The administration policy is similar to that called "constructive engagement" with respect to overall relations with South Africa. The administration's rationale for such "constructive engagement" in the nuclear area was that a modest level of nuclear trade could help the United States start a serious dialogue with these countries on broader proliferation questions. The nuclear industry, anxious to restore the U.S. image as a reliable nuclear supplier, holds the same views.

However, when word of some "constructive engagement" transactions concerning the sale to South Africa of equipment that contained Helium-3 for testing nuclear fuel and the retransfer of U.S.-origin heavy water from Europe to Argentina became known to congressional staff experts and to a handful of key reporters for the *New York Times*, the *Washington Post*, and the trade journal *Nucleonics Week*, an uproar ensued in Congress. Congressional opponents of this policy argued that even though existing legislation did not specifically outlaw such component exports, the U.S. should not help these countries with their nuclear programs in any way. Congressional staffers brought the transactions to the attention of their senators and representatives, recommending that hearings be held or that legislation be introduced to prevent the administration from pursuing its more liberal export policy.

By the fall of 1983, after the announcement that nuclear components would be exported to India and heavy water transferred to Argentina, congressional opposition had grown fairly strong. Unfortunately, many of the legislators most expert in non-proliferation issues were missing from the scene. Congressman Bingham had retired, and Senators Glenn, Cranston, and Hart were campaigning for the Democratic presidential nomination. That meant that the job of amending the Nuclear Non-Proliferation Act fell to legislators (and staff) with considerably less background in the field. Outside experts, particularly the Nuclear Control Institute, helped them refine their proposals. Despite heavy lobbying by the Reagan administration and the nuclear industry (through its lobby group, the American Nuclear Energy Council), the legislation passed by a large margin in both houses of Congress as part of the 1984 Export Administration Law.

That is not the end of the story, however. The bill died in late 1984 in conference committee, where members of the House and Senate meet to work out differences between their two versions of a proposed law. Because the two houses could not agree on various other features of the bill, it languished in committee until the end of the 98th Congress. Any bill that doesn't get out of committee and sent to the Congress for a vote on final passage by the end of a congressional session dies a natural death. The new Congress elected in the fall does not have the same composition and does not consider left-over bills unless they are introduced again. Whether or not this bill will be introduced again in 1985 or there-after is still uncertain as we go to press.

This episode shows the interplay of forces through which policy is made. The administration wanted to pur-sue a more lenient policy with respect to exports to certain potential proliferators. The Congress strongly disagreed with the administration approach and attempted to outlaw it by passing legislative strictures not expli-citly stated in the initial act (though the legislation was bottled up in committee as noted above). Key roles in the drama were played by the press and lobbying groups like the Nuclear Control Institute and the American Nu-clear Energy Council.

The ways in which individual citizens can have an impact on the making of such policy are the same ones you learned about in high school civics: Our country is a representative democracy, and the opinions of citizens count, both in the voting booth and between elections in various forums. The legislative process recounted above resulted in two key votes. Citizens can weigh in with their opinions by sending letters and telegrams to their senators and representatives. House members virtually hit the ground running after each election, since they must face another one in two years' time, so they are particularly sensitive to constituents' views. Senators can afford to be somewhat less responsive, since they face campaigns at only six-year intervals and might be able to count on a loss in short-term voter memory be-tween elections.

Another way for citizens to take action is to join with community groups that meet to study the issue, make recommendations to their legislators, and plan activities to increase public awareness about proliferation. The United Nations Association mounted an intensive educa-tional effort along these lines in 1983-84, in which hundreds of citizens first studied a briefing book to educate themselves about the complexities of the subject and then met to propose options, all of which were then gathered together and published in a second booklet. Most such groups will take a nonpartisan, non-advocacy approach to the subject and will be very careful to maintain that balanced posture.

Citizens who want to take an advocacy role can amplify their voices by joining in with like-minded lobby groups. The American Nuclear Energy Council and the American Nuclear Society represent the views of the nuclear industry. Some individual exporters, such as Westinghouse, are also active lobbyists. On the other side are the Nuclear Control Institute and the Natural Resources Defense Council, Inc., both nonprofit groups supported by foundations and members. All these groups have offices in Washington, D.C., and would be happy to hear from you. (Names and addresses of various groups appear in Appendix I.)

Last Words

These accounts were, by design, chosen to present differing points of view about how best to deal with the problem of proliferation. As we said at the outset, we make no claim to know the answers. That is an exercise for the reader, after having weighed the options and examined the evidence.

We would, however, like to tell one more story, in an attempt to heighten the urgency we hope you now feel about finding ways to solve the proliferation puzzle. We want you to know in advance that we have stolen the structure from John Fowles' *The French Lieutenant's Woman*. The Epilogue is thus not one ending, but two. We want to show that even *after* the hypothetical death of Washington chronicled in the Prologue, the world could take two very different paths, one leading to despair and the other to hope.

We hope this book and the efforts of others in the field will help to create a human wave of concern about the problem so that governments will be irresistibly moved toward finding serious ways to deal with it. We would like to be as wrong about prospects for the world of 1996--the story in the Prologue--as George Orwell was about those for 1984, and for the same reasons. It is arguable that worry about the worst-case scenario can translate into action to prevent it, with enough success that thirty years later the fear that was the spring to action can hardly be understood by the new generation which inherits a changed world.

EPILOGUE: AUGUST 6, 2016

DOOM

I was twelve when Washington got blown up. It was twenty years ago today. We lived seventy miles away in the Blue Ridge Mountains and the next morning we went a lot farther. We tried to take our neighbor, an old lady who was my friend, with us but she wouldn't leave. A hundred miles into West Virginia. It seemed like a long way at the time. I wish there were still someplace safe to go, however far. It was hard being a kid then. It's harder to think about having one now.

My family moved out of Washington five years before the bomb. It's not as though they knew to save us or anything. Nobody expected that bomb. Nobody was even scared then; people thought things had gotten better.

There were people who even thought things would somehow be all right after Washington. We got pretty thick with the Soviets, even had a joint SWAT team that tracked down terrorists all over the world and found a bomb in Moscow before it could go off. For a few years we were doing this grotesque dance together, almost allies. We looked pretty good to each other next to the other people who might get the bomb. So we tried to put a lid on it. But we didn't do enough. We couldn't get along well enough to.

We're still trying, but the world isn't working out like we wanted. We thought we could keep it us and them forever, a sort of Thousand-Year Cold War. With us two in control, once we finally gave up on burying each other. We thought we were ahead of the game. Until the game changed and we couldn't stop it.

There are twenty countries with the bomb now, and some of them have been enemies for a thousand years. There are on-again, off-again regional wars on three continents. India and Pakistan have gotten close to the abyss more than once. So far they've always pulled back in time. The closest call was two months ago. The only hope you can have is that everybody's as scared as we and the Soviets are.

And that's plenty scared. The nuclear winter stuff

has been around a long time, since the 1980s. The numbers keep getting refined downward while the number of people who've got the bomb grows. Best guess now is that if India and Pakistan had let fly with all they had last June, a hundred cities would have gone up in smoke. Enough to spread darkness and cold over the Northern Hemisphere until October at least, and maybe the Southern Hemisphere, too. And maybe for longer. The guesses on how long it would last are pretty tenuous. What plant life might survive, whether the oceans might die, whether air might even be in short supply--these are the stuff of wild speculation. But mass famine is certain enough. If it happens. Like some expert said, we might know fifty percent of the effects of nuclear war, but that won't keep a hundred percent of them from happening.

There's a building boom undergound, whole survivalist communities with little tombs they can live in, whatever befalls the earth. Makes the bomb shelters of the 1950s look sane. Nobody knew then that the earth might die with us.

If it didn't--and we didn't--what would climb out of the ground at last? I can't think the species that might survive would be mine. We were shrews in the last Ice Age, blessedly lacking in memory and foresight. Will anything recognizably human survive another one? Depends on what you think is human, I guess. And how bad a hundred percent of the effects turns out to be. And whether there's more than one war at a time.

Sometimes at the ocean it's possible to forget how awful the world is. It's getting harder to manage that all the time, but for a few minutes this afternoon I forgot. Lying on the beach in the sun can burn out all the fear, for a while. The sand molds to your body and bears you up. You feel at home in the world. The earth as mother. It's hard to see how a whole species that once thought that way about the earth could have come to this.

I even forgot the real reason I came here. But it came back with a jolt. Sometimes I want this baby, no matter what. Even if I don't think the world has a future. I haven't told my husband yet. He'll want it, no question. I have to know what I can live with first. How I can live at all, no matter what I choose. I could swim out toward the horizon. Take arms against a sea of troubles and so end them. Except it's so cowardly, and I've been brave for a long time.

My younger brother can't remember a time when he wasn't afraid, when he didn't wonder if the world would last until morning. Only people at least as old as I am can remember what it was like to be a kid and think you were immortal.

I've got two more days here. And then I have to know. My body wants this child, always has. Maybe I'll just go with it, blindly. There's no way to know what will happen. Maybe the world will last after all. If it's going to end anyway, I wish it would happen now. Whatever it is. I could take it better alone.

In the midst of life we are in death. As has always been the case, but never like this before. We owe the world a death. But it's supposed to be our own. Instead, the mortality of the world hangs over us while we scan the newspapers, look for omens, try to make a life that makes sense in a time that doesn't, that could, in fact, run out.

In the midst of death I am in life. With child. If I can find it in me to think we'll beat the odds.

BLOOM

It happened twenty years ago today. My family lived in the Blue Ridge Mountains and Washington was seventy miles away. What I remember is the flash of light, the noise, how scared I was. I was twelve years old and I thought it was the end of the world. My little brother got to my parents' bed first. As if they could help.

I remember screaming and my mother shaking me so I would stop. And then she held me fiercely and after a while she started singing songs like when I was little. It worked for my littler brother. To this day, I can't hear "Amazing Grace" or "Greensleeves" without a sense of that distant roar on the horizon.

My parents mostly told me the truth, so when they started saying things I didn't think they believed, I got even more scared. But I did the same thing with my little brother.

I remember they went from "There won't be any bombs close to us" to "There won't be any more bombs." And I from being glad we were so far away from Washington to feeling awful about the people who weren't. Even my old lady friend tried to hide the truth from me. Anyway, I didn't believe it was over. It took days, weeks even, before I stopped expecting to get blown up every second. I wondered if I'd live to be thirteen. I'm thirty-two now, and it looks as though Washington was the last nuclear war.

Odd that what I thought was the end was a beginning instead. I'm a little fuzzy on the details. Somehow America and the Soviets put together a sort of nuclear SWAT team, virtually overnight. In fact, for some years there had been an intelligence pact between them so secret that only a handful of people on both sides knew about it. If they had really gotten together sooner they might have saved Washington. A couple of days later and they would have lost Moscow too. There were raids in six countries at once. The SWAT team got all the terrorists, and the Moscow bomb.

Moscow was supposed to blow when Washington did, the papers said. There was some trouble with the Moscow bomb; it didn't go off on time. The terrorists were trying to fix it when the SWAT team got them. I remember when the story broke. I still have the front page with the four-inch-high headline. I remember people being sorry that Moscow got the dud bomb, instead of Washington. But nobody said it in public. Not once they knew what a near miss it was.

After that, a lot of things happened pretty quickly. There was a new President and Congress, and the capital was Philadelphia. There was a summit meeting that went on for months. The superpower SWAT team made a couple more raids.

The Middle East peace treaty was signed the next year, mediated by the United States and the Soviet Union. Southern Africa was the hardest. But even that was settled. Latin America was easy by comparison.

They say there won't be much left of any of the armies before long. Too expensive, and we don't need them now that the planet has settled down. The borders are frozen and we're teaching the kids that it will be that way forever. It's funny for them to learn about all those other maps, other countries.

We don't talk much about the bomb anymore. Oh, maybe we'll listen in now and then when they're announcing a new treaty. There are still a lot of bombs around but the numbers go down every year and no one mines uranium anymore. Worth watching, but not worrying about.

What used to be the center of Washington got left in ruins, and after a while the kudzu took it over, the bushy vines giving such thick cover that you can barely guess at the broken shapes beneath. A monument of another sort. People from all over the world come to see. Nobody talks much. I came here for the first time today. There are walkways and a map, but not much that you can recognize. A greenish glass crater that used to be Lafayette Square. The base of the Washington Monument. A piece of the Vietnam wall. The names are still there. You can climb down into a sort of crypt and see the Bill of Rights and the Constitution. A chunk of marble with a few of Jefferson's words: "Justice cannot sleep forever." The empty hulk of Saint Matthew's Cathedral. And everywhere the kudzu.

The Potomac is alight with paper lanterns, like it is every year on this night. The Japanese taught us how. You have to look back in sorrow, even if the peace we have made is worth what it cost. It will be easier to think about once there is no living memory of the price, the shadows on stone in the ruined capital, the people dying still. I'd like to think that Washington will stand like this for a thousand years, a warning and a signpost. A crossroads stone for when the world woke up.

APPENDIX A
Text of the Treaty on the Non-Proliferation of Nuclear Weapons

Signed at Washington, London, and Moscow, July 1, 1968
Ratification advised by U.S. Senate March 13, 1969
Ratified by U.S. President November 24, 1969
U.S. ratification deposited at Washington, London, and Moscow March 5, 1970
Proclaimed by U.S. President March 5, 1970
Entered into force March 5, 1970

Article I

Each nuclear-weapon State Party to the Treaty undertakes not to transfer to any recipient whatsoever nuclear weapons or other nuclear explosive devices or control over such weapons or explosive devices directly, or indirectly, and not in any way to assist, encourage, or induce any non-nuclear-weapon State to manufacture or otherwise acquire nuclear weapons or other nuclear explosive devices, or control over such weapons or explosive devices.

Article II

Each non-nuclear-weapon State Party to the Treaty undertakes not to receive the transfer from any transferor whatsoever of nuclear weapons or other nuclear explosive devices or of control over such weapons or explosive devices directly, or indirectly; not to manufacture or otherwise acquire nuclear weapons or other nuclear explosive devices; and not to seek or receive any assistance in the manufacture of nuclear weapons or other nuclear explosive devices.

Article III

1. Each non-nuclear-weapon State Party to the Treaty undertakes to accept safeguards, as set forth in an agreement to be negotiated and concluded with the International Atomic Energy Agency in accordance with the Statute of the International Atomic Energy Agency and the Agency's safeguards system, for the exclusive purpose of verification of the fulfillment of its obligations assumed under this Treaty with a view to preventing diversion of nuclear energy from peaceful uses to nuclear weapons or other nuclear explosive devices. Procedures for the safeguards required by this article shall be followed with respect to source or special fissionable

material whether it is being produced, processed or used in any principal nuclear facility or is outside any such facility. The safeguards required by this article shall be applied to all source or special fissionable material in all peaceful nuclear activities within the territory of such State, under its jurisdiction, or carried out under its control anywhere.

2. Each State Party to the Treaty undertakes not to provide: (a) source or special fissionable material, or (b) equipment or material especially designed or prepared for the processing, use or production of special fissionable material, to any non-nuclear-weapon State for peaceful purposes, unless the source or special fissionable material shall be subject to the safeguards required by this article.

3. The safeguards required by this article shall be implemented in a manner designed to comply with article IV of this Treaty, and to avoid hampering the economic or technological development of the Parties or international cooperation in the field of peaceful nuclear activities, including the international exchange of nuclear material and equipment for the processing, use or production of nuclear material for peaceful purposes in accordance with the provisions of this article and the principle of safeguarding set forth in the Preamble of the Treaty.

4. Non-nuclear-weapon States Party to the Treaty shall conclude agreements with the International Atomic Energy Agency to meet the requirements of this article either individually or together with other States in accordance with the Statute of the International Atomic Energy Agency. Negotiation of such agreements shall commence within 180 days from the original entry into force of this Treaty. For States depositing their instruments of ratification or accession after the 180-day period, negotiation of such agreements shall commence not later than the date of such deposit. Such agreements shall enter into force not later than eighteen months after the date of initiation of negotiations.

Article IV

1. Nothing in this Treaty shall be interpreted as affecting the inalienable right of all the Parties to the Treaty to develop research, production and use of nuclear energy for peaceful purposes without discrimination and in conformity with articles I and II of this Treaty.

2. All the Parties to the Treaty undertake to facilitate, and have the right to participate in, the fullest possible exchange of equipment, materials and scientific and technological information for the peaceful uses of nuclear energy. Parties to the Treaty in a position to do so shall also cooperate in contributing alone or together with other States or international organizations to the further development of the applications of nuclear energy for peaceful purposes, especially in the territories of non-nuclear-weapon States Party to the Treaty, with due consideration for

the needs of the developing areas of the world.

Article V

Each Party to the Treaty undertakes to take appropriate measures to ensure that, in accordance with this Treaty, under appropriate international observation and through appropriate international procedures, potential benefits from any peaceful applications of nuclear explosions will be made available to non-nuclear-weapons States Party to the Treaty on a nondiscriminatory basis and that the charge to such Parties for the explosive devices used will be as low as possible and exclude any charge for research and development. Non-nuclear-weapon States Party to the Treaty shall be able to obtain such benefits, pursuant to a special international agreement or agreements, through an appropriate international body with adequate representation of non-nuclear-weapon States. Negotiations on this subject shall commence as soon as possible after the Treaty enters into force. Non-nuclear-weapon States Party to the Treaty so desiring may also obtain such benefits pursuant to bilateral agreements.

Article VI

Each of the Parties to the Treaty undertakes to pursue negotiations in good faith on effective measures relating to cessation of the nuclear arms race at an early date and to nuclear disarmament, and on a treaty on general and complete disarmament under strict and effective international control.

Article VII

Nothing in this Treaty affects the right of any group of States to conclude regional treaties in order to assure the total absence of nuclear weapons in their respective territories.

Article VIII

1. Any Party to the Treaty may propose amendments to this Treaty. The text of any proposed amendment shall be submitted to the Depositary Governments which shall circulate it to all Parties to the Treaty. Thereupon, if requested to do so by one-third or more of the Parties to the Treaty, the Depositary Governments shall convene a conference, to which they shall invite all the Parties to the Treaty, to consider such an amendment.

2. Any amendment to this Treaty must be approved by a majority of the votes of all the Parties to the Treaty, including the votes of all nuclear-weapon States Party to the Treaty and all other Parties which, on the date

the amendment is circulated, are members of the Board of Governors of the International Atomic Energy Agency. The amendment shall enter into force for each Party that deposits its instrument of ratification of the amendment upon the deposit of such instruments of ratification by a majority of all the Parties, including the instruments of ratification of all nuclear-weapon States Party to the Treaty and all other Parties which, on the date the amendment is circulated, are members of the Board of Governors of the International Atomic Energy Agency. Thereafter, it shall enter into force for any other Party upon the deposit of its instrument of ratification of the amendment.

3. Five years after the entry into force of this Treaty, a conference of Parties to the Treaty shall be held in Geneva, Switzerland, in order to review the operation of this Treaty with a view to assuring that the purposes of the Preamble and the provisions of the Treaty are being realized. At intervals of five years thereafter, a majority of the Parties to the Treaty may obtain, by submitting a proposal to this effect to the Depositary Governments, the convening of further conferences with the same objective of reviewing the operation of the Treaty.

Article IX

1. This Treaty shall be open to all States for signature. Any State which does not sign the Treaty before its entry into force in accordance with paragraph 3 of this article may accede to it at any time.

2. This Treaty shall be subject to ratification by signatory States. Instruments of ratification and instruments of accession shall be deposited with the Governments of the United States of America, the United Kingdom of Great Britain and Northern Ireland and the Union of Soviet Socialist Republics, which are hereby designated the Depositary Governments.

3. This Treaty shall enter into force after its ratification by the States, the Governments of which are designated Depositaries of the Treaty, and forty other States signatory to this Treaty and the deposit of their instruments of ratification. For the purposes of this Treaty, a nuclear-weapon State is one which has manufactured and exploded a nuclear weapon or other nuclear explosive device prior to January 1, 1967.

4. For States whose instruments of ratification or accession are deposited subsequent to the entry into force of this Treaty, it shall enter into force on the date of the deposit of their instruments of ratification or accession.

5. The Depositary Governments shall promptly inform all signatory and acceding States of the date of each signature, the date of deposit of each instrument of ratification or of accession, the date of the entry into force of this Treaty, and the date of receipt of any requests for convening a conference or other notices.

6. This Treaty shall be registered by the Depositary Governments pursuant to article 102 of the Charter of the United Nations.

Article X

1. Each Party shall in exercising its national sovereignty have the right to withdraw from the Treaty if it decides that extraordinary events, related to the subject matter of this Treaty, have jeopardized the supreme interests of its country. It shall give notice of such withdrawal to all other Parties to the Treaty and to the United Nations Security Council three months in advance. Such notice shall include a statement of the extraordinary events it regards as having jeopardized its supreme interests.

2. Twenty-five years after the entry into force of the Treaty, a conference shall be convened to decide whether the Treaty shall continue in force indefinitely, or shall be extended for an additional fixed period or periods. This decision shall be taken by a majority of the Parties to the Treaty.

Article XI

This Treaty, the English, Russian, French, Spanish and Chinese texts of which are equally authentic, shall be deposited in the archives of the Depositary Governments. Duly certified copies of this Treaty shall be transmitted by the Depositary Governments to the Governments of the signatory and acceding States.

IN WITNESS WHEREOF the undersigned, duly authorized, have signed this Treaty.

DONE in triplicate, at the cities of Washington, London and Moscow, this first day of July one thousand nine hundred sixty-eight.

Parties to the Non-Proliferation Treaty

Afghanistan
Antigua and Barbuda[1]
Australia
Austria
Bahamas, The
Bangladesh
Barbados
Belgium
Benin
Bolivia
Botswana
Brunei
Bulgaria
Burundi
Cameroon
Canada
Cape Verde
Central African
  Republic
Chad
Congo
Costa Rica
Cyprus
Czechoslovakia
Denmark
Dominica
Dominican Republic
Ecuador
Egypt
El Salvador
Equatorial Guinea
Ethiopia
Fiji
Finland
Gabon
Gambia, The
German Democratic
  Republic
Germany, Federal
  Republic of
Ghana
Greece

Grenada
Guatemala
Guinea-Bissau
Haiti
Holy See
Honduras
Hungary
Iceland
Indonesia
Iran
Iraq
Ireland
Italy
Ivory Coast
Jamaica
Japan
Jordan
Kampuchea
Kenya
Korea, Republic of
Laos
Lebanon
Lesotho
Liberia
Libya
Liechtenstein
Luxembourg
Madagascar
Malaysia
Maldives
Mali
Malta
Mauritius
Mexico
Mongolia
Morocco
Nauru
Nepal
Netherlands
New Zealand
Nicaragua
Nigeria

[1] Based on general declarations concerning continuing Treaty obligations applicable prior to independence.

WHO WILL STOP THE BOMB?

Norway
Panama
Papua New Guinea
Paraguay
Peru
Philippines
Poland
Portugal
Romania
Rwanda
St. Christopher
  and Nevis[1]
St. Lucia
St. Vincent and
  the Grenadines
Sao Tome and Principe
San Marino
Senegal
Sierra Leone
Singapore
Solomon Islands
Somalia
Sri Lanka
Sudan
Suriname
Swaziland
Sweden

Switzerland
Syrian Arab Republic
Taiwan
Thailand
Togo
Tongo
Tunisia
Turkey
Tuvalu
Uganda
Union of Soviet
  Socialist Republics
United Kingdom
United States
Upper Volta
  (now Burkina Faso)
Uruguay
Venezuela
Vietnam, Socialist
  Republic of
Western Samoa
Yemen, People's
  Democratic
  Republic of
Yugoslavia
Zaire

[1] Based on general declarations concerning continuing Treaty obligations
applicable prior to independence.

APPENDIX B
Nuclear Status of Problem Countries

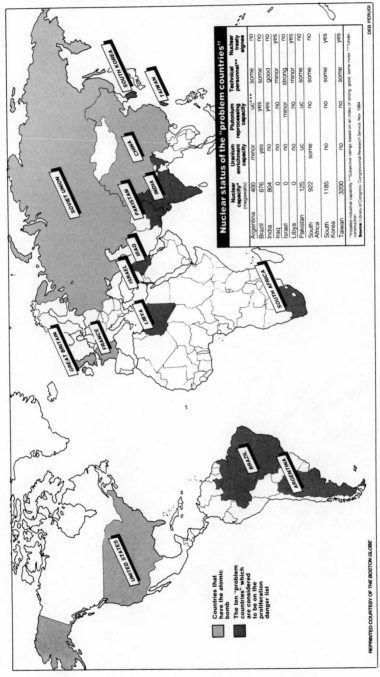

Nuclear status of the "problem countries"

	Nuclear capacity* (megawatts)	Uranium enrichment capacity	Plutonium reprocessing capacity	Technical personnel**	Nuclear treaty signee
Argentina	400	minor	uc***	some	no
Brazil	676	yes	yes	some	no
India	804	no	yes	good	no
Iraq	0	no	no	minor	yes
Israel	0	no	no	strong	no
Libya	0	no	minor	minor	yes
Pakistan	125	no	no	some	no
South Africa	922	some	uc	uc	no
South Korea	1185	no	no	some	yes
Taiwan	3200	no	no	some	yes

*Installed industrial capability ***Subjective ratings based on an index of strong, good, some, minor ***Under construction
Source: Library of Congress Congressional Research Service, Nov. 1984

Countries that have the atomic bomb

The ten "problem countries" which are considered to be on the proliferation danger list

DEB PERUGI

APPENDIX C
Countries with Nuclear Power Plants

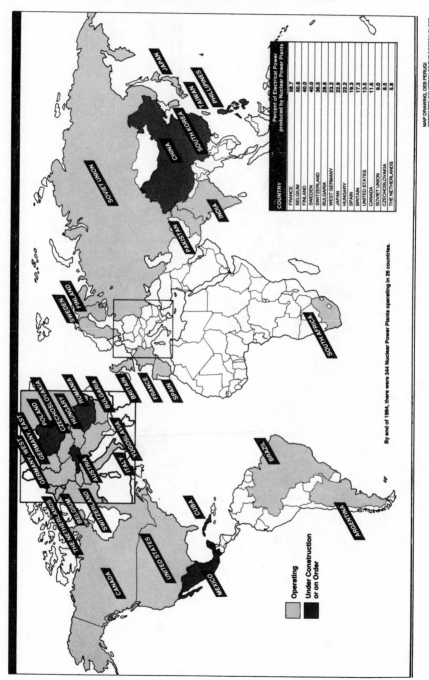

COUNTRY	Percent of Electrical Power produced by Nuclear Power Plants
FRANCE	58.7
BELGIUM	50.8
FINLAND	40.0
SWEDEN	40.0
SWITZERLAND	36.5
BULGARIA	28.6
WEST GERMANY	23.2
JAPAN	22.9
HUNGARY	22.2
SPAIN	19.3
BRITAIN	17.3
UNITED STATES	13.5
CANADA	11.6
SOVIET UNION	9.0
CZECHOSLOVAKIA	8.5
THE NETHERLANDS	5.8

Operating

Under Construction or on Order

By end of 1984, there were 344 Nuclear Power Plants operating in 26 countries.

MAP DRAWING, DEB PERUGI
REPRINTED COURTESY OF THE BOSTON GLOBE
ADDITIONAL ARTWORK, MICHELLE HIGGINS

APPENDIX D
Uranium-Producing Countries

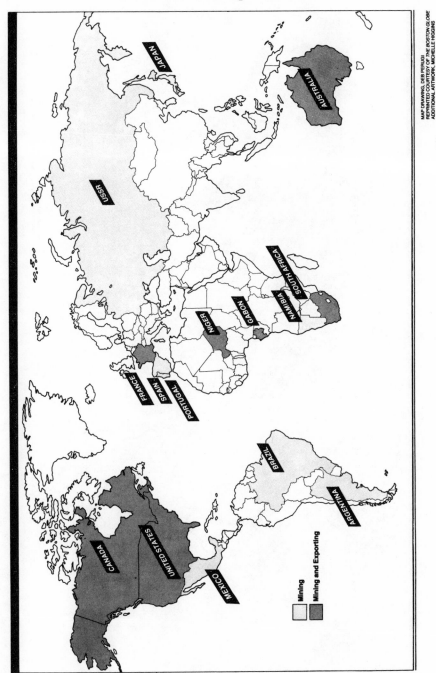

MAP DRAWING, DEB PERUGI
REPRINTED COURTESY OF THE BOSTON GLOBE
ADDITIONAL ARTWORK, MICHELLE HIGGINS

JAPAN

AUSTRALIA

USSR

SOUTH AFRICA

NAMIBIA

GABON

NIGER

FRANCE

SPAIN

PORTUGAL

BRAZIL

ARGENTINA

CANADA

UNITED STATES

MEXICO

Mining

Mining and Exporting

APPENDIX E
Plutonium-Reprocessing Countries

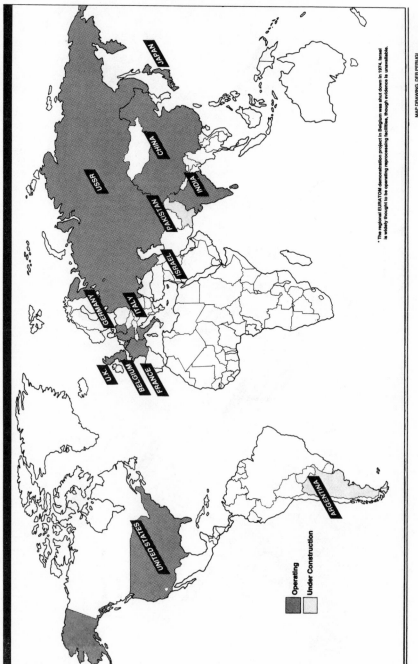

Operating

Under Construction

* The regional EURATOM demonstration project in Belgium was shut down in 1974. Israel is widely thought to be operating reprocessing facilities, though evidence is unavailable.

MAP DRAWING, DEB PERUGI
REPRINTED COURTESY OF THE BOSTON GLOBE
ADDITIONAL ARTWORK, MICHELLE HIGGINS

APPENDIX F

SOURCES

"Americans May be Working Illegally at South African Reactor." *The Washington Post,* Jan. 20, 1985.

"Argentina Develops Its Own Nuclear Facilities, But National Austerity Hampers the Program." *Wall Street Journal,* Nov. 29, 1984.

Arms Control and Disarmament Agreements. Washington, D.C.: United States Arms Control and Disarmament Agency, 1982.

Barasch, Marc. *The Little Black Book of Atomic War.* New York: Dell, 1983.

Carnesale, Albert, et al. *Living with Nuclear Weapons.* New York: Bantam Books, 1983.

"Desert Military, Blacks Urged: Qaddafi Speaks to Meeting of Muslims in Chicago." *The Washington Post,* Feb. 25, 1985.

Greenwood, Ted, Harold A. Feiveson, and Theodore B. Taylor. *Nuclear Proliferation: Motivations, Capabilities, and Strategies for Control.* Council on Foreign Relations, 1980s Project. New York: McGraw-Hill, 1979.

--,George W. Rathjens, and Jack Ruina. *Nuclear Power and Weapons Proliferation.* Adelphi Paper No. 130. London: The International Institute for Strategic Studies, 1977.

"How Pakistan Secured U.S. Devices in Canada to Make Atomic Arms." *Wall Street Journal,* Nov. 26, 1984.

"India, Keeping its Nuclear Options Open, Monitors Arms Program in Neighboring Pakistan with Concern." *Wall Street Journal,* Nov. 27, 1984.

"Israel Pointedly Avoids Discussing Nuclear Weapons, But Western Officials Suspect It Has a Small Arsenal." *Wall Street Journal,* Nov. 27, 1984.

Kohn, Howard, and Barbara Newman. "How Israel Got the Nuclear Bomb." *Rolling Stone,* Dec. 1, 1977: 38-40.

"Laser Offers Cut-Price Nuclear Fuel--And More Proliferation?" *The Economist,* June 30, 1984: 71-72.

"New Zealand Premier Reports New U.S. Moves." *The Washington Post,* Feb. 20, 1985.

Nuclear Proliferation: A Citizen's Guide to Policy Choices. Multilateral Project. New York: United Nations Association of the U.S., 1983.

Nuclear Proliferation and Safeguards. Washington, D.C.: Congress of the United States, Office of Technology Assessment, 1977.

"Nuclear Nonproliferation Effort is Hampered by Patchwork of Controls, Need for Consensus." *Wall Street Journal*, Nov. 30, 1984.

Nye, Joseph S. "To Manage is Human; To Prevent, Divine." *Society*, vol. 20, Sept./Oct, 1983.

"South Africa Has Technology and Manpower to Make Nuclear Weapons--but for What?" *Wall Street Journal*, Nov. 28, 1984.

Spector, Leonard S. "Non-Proliferation: The Reagan Record." *Arms Control Today*, January 1985: 2-3, 10-11, 13.

--.*Nuclear Proliferation Today.* New York: Vintage Books, 1984.

--.*The Other Nuclear Arms Race.* Manuscript, to be published by The Roosevelt Center, 1985.

"The Good War: An Oral History of World War Two." (rev.) *New York Times Book Review*, Oct. 7, 1984.

The Present Challenge: A Report on the Nuclear Dilemma. Cox Newspapers, April 10, 1983.

"Wave of Terror Stirs Anxiety Across Europe." *The Washington Post*, Feb. 10, 1985.

Weart, Spencer R. *Scientists in Power.* Cambridge: Harvard University Press, 1979.

Wyden, Peter. *Day One: Before Hiroshima and After.* New York: Simon & Schuster, 1984.

Zuckerman, Edward. *The Day After World War III.* New York: Viking Press, 1984.

APPENDIX G

Notes

CHAPTER ONE

Theodore Taylor quoted: Barasch, 40.

Categories of terrorist groups: Greenwood, (*Nuclear Proliferation: Motivations, Capabilities, and Strategies for Control*, 99-101.

Savannah River mock assault: Spector (*The Other Nuclear Arms Race*).

Breaking taboo itself powerful incitement: Greenwood, *Nuclear Proliferation*, 100.

Khomeini speech: *Harper's*, April 1985, p. 17.

Revival of European terrorism: *The Washington Post*, Feb. 10, 1985.

H. G. Wells quoted: Weart, 209.

Special Committee on Atomic Energy hearing quoted: Barasch, 39.

CHAPTER TWO

J. Robert Oppenheimer quoted: Barasch, 12.

Albert Einstein quoted: Zuckerman, 25.

French scientists first to split the atom: Weart. 57-59.

Concern about "chance of grave misuse in Europe": Weart, 87.

CIA estimate "at least 50 countries will have the capability to develop nuclear weapons": Cox Newspapers, 21.

ABC promotional poster quoted: Barasch, 17.

Breeder reactor 50-100 times more efficient using uranium, fuel pellets could be turned directly into bombs: *Nuclear Proliferation: A Citizen's Guide to Policy Choices*, 19.

4,000 stages for gaseous diffusion enrichment to weapons-grade, 35 stages for centrifuge: Greenwood, *Nuclear Power and Weapons Proliferation*, 23.

CHAPTER THREE

Argentina agreed to pay West Germany and Switzerland a half billion dollars more than Canada would have charged for reactor: Spector, *The Other Nuclear Arms Race.*

Suppliers secret meeting in Luxembourg: *Wall Street Journal*, Nov. 30, 1984.

CHAPTER FOUR

United States

Eisenhower's opposition to bomb-drop decision: Zuckerman, 37.

Manhattan Project scientists' opposition to bomb-drop decision: Zuckerman, 37-39.

"Harry dropped that beautiful bomb" quoted in rev. of *The Good War*, Studs Terkel, *New York Times Book Review* Oct. 7, 1984.

Stalin's comment "atomic bomb not a serious force": quoted in Barasch, 21.

Truman-Oppenheimer exchange on when Russians will be able to build the bomb: Cox Newspapers, 3.

Soviet Union

Emelyanov's comment "They would have shot us": quoted in Barasch, 14.

Fuch's comment "I had complete confidence in Russian policy": quoted in Wyden, 89.

Soviet bomb building progress: Wyden, 89-90.

Britain

Impetus to build the bomb: OTA, 98-99.

Clement Attlee "...we'd got to show them that they didn't know everything": quoted in Barasch, 14.

France

Impetus to build the bomb: OTA, 100-101.

Szilard comment on Joliot "...he might have beaten us to it": quoted in Weart, 150.

"He wanted to change France's reputation": quoted in Barasch, 14.

China

Impetus, who helped: OTA, 101-102.

CHAPTER FIVE

Except where otherwise noted, facts come from Spector, *Nuclear Proliferation Today.*

India

Spector, *Nuclear Proliferation Today*, 23-63.

Soviet response to Indian test: OTA.

Subrahmanyam quote, Roosevelt Center interview, October, 1984.

Israel

Spector, *Nuclear Proliferation Today*, 117-148.

"Every country has its own sin": telephone interview, November 1984.

NUMEC story: *Rolling Stone*, Dec. 1, 1977.

CSIS study: *Wall Street Journal*, Nov. 27, 1984.

South Africa

Spector, *Nuclear Proliferation Today*, 279-307.

Koeberg reactor complex, Subcommittee on African Affairs hearing: Cox Newspapers, 27-28.

Americans reportedly working at Koeberg: *Washington Post*, Jan. 20, 1985.

Pakistan

Spector, *Nuclear Proliferation Today*, 70-106.

Bhutto comment "we will get one of our own": quoted in Barasch, 14.

Pakistanis arrested in Canada, Chinese technicians helping: *Wall Street Journal*, Nov. 26, 1984.

Kahn comment "cannot make a good bicycle...": *Wall Street Journal*, Nov. 26, 1984.

Sen. Cranston assertion that Kahn centrifuge unit may be able to produce enough enriched uranium for one atomic bomb a year: Spector, "Non-Proliferation: The Reagan Record," 2.

Pakistani arrested in Houston for trying to smuggle out electronic switches: Seymour Hersh, *Frontline*, March 5, 1985.

CHAPTER SIX

Unless otherwise noted, facts come from Spector, *Nuclear Proliferation Today.*

Argentina

Spector, *Nuclear Proliferation Today*, 199-230.

Impetus to build the bomb: OTA, 103-104.

"Impossible to have any more surprise projects": *Wall Street Journal*, Nov. 25, 1984.

CRS estimate that reprocessing plant could produce plutonium for ten atomic bombs a year: Cox Newspapers, 24.

Brazil

Spector, *Nuclear Proliferation Today*, 235-259.

Iraq

Spector, *Nuclear Proliferation Today*, 165-188.

Hussein comment "assist the Arabs in one way or another...": Spector, *The Other Nuclear Arms Race.*

Libya

Spector, *Nuclear Proliferation Today*, 149-162.

Qaddafi's comment "we shall be able to buy an atomic bomb": quoted in Barasch, 16.

Qaddafi's speech to Muslim conference: *The Washington Post*, Feb. 25, 1985.

Aftermath in IAEA of Israeli Osirak raid: *Nuclear Proliferation: A Citizen's Guide to Policy Choices.*

South Korea

Spector, *The Other Nuclear Arms Race.*

Taiwan

Impetus to build the bomb: OTA, 108-109.

Spector, *The Other Nuclear Arms Race.*

CHAPTER SEVEN

D. H. Lawrence comment on World War I, "All the great words were cancelled out": Quoted in Tuchman, *The Guns of August*, 489.

George Schultz comment "New Zealand has basically taken a walk...": *Washington Post*, Feb. 20, 1985.

CHAPTER EIGHT

Szilard epigraph "it will appear to many people premature to take some action": quoted in Weart, 77.

Discussion of U.S. policy making: Spector, *The Other Nuclear Arms Race.*

Four Horsemen against the apocalypse: Personal interviews conducted by Christopher Makins, Summer 1984.

APPENDIX A

Reprinted from ACDA document, *Arms Control and Disarmament Agreements.* Washington, D.C.: 1982.

APPENDIX H

SUGGESTIONS FOR FURTHER READING

Nuclear Proliferation Today. By Leonard S. Spector. A Carnegie Endowment Book. New York: Vintage, 1984.

First in a series of Carnegie Endowment annual reports on proliferation, this report is available in bookstores in hard cover and paperback editions. Easily the most comprehensive treatment extant of non-proliferation on a country-by-country basis.

Nuclear Proliferation and Safeguards. By the U.S. Congress' Office of Technology Assessment, 1977. Can be ordered from the Commerce Department's National Technical Information Service (document number PB 275843; cost $22.00). (703) 655-4000.

The volume is a technical survey and includes valuable charts and tables. Somewhat dated, but useful.

Nuclear Proliferation: Motivations, Capabilities, and Strategies for Control. By Ted Greenwood, Harold A. Feiveson, and Theodore B. Taylor. Council on Foreign Relations 1980s Project. New York: McGraw-Hill, 1979.

The library might be the best place to look for this volume, though it is probably available at specialized book stores as well. An excellent survey of the field by three scientists, well written and not excessively technical.

Nuclear Proliferation: A Citizen's Guide to Policy Choices and *Nuclear Proliferation: Toward Global Restraint.*

Both booklets are products of the U.N. Association's Multilateral Project and figured in its nine-month study conducted in 1983-84, involving hundreds of concerned citizens. The first is a 48-page booklet researched and written by Ann Florini, which lays out facts and policy options, giving valuable reading lists at the end of each section. The second gathers together the recommendations put forth by the citizens' groups after they had studied the matter. Available from the U.N. Association, 300 East 42nd Street, New York, New York 10017.

Controlling the Bomb: Nuclear Proliferation in the 1980s. By Lewis A. Dunn. New York, Yale University Press, 1982.

An excellent and readable survey of the field.

APPENDIX I

ORGANIZATIONS WORKING THE FIELD

American Nuclear Energy
Council
410 First Street, S.E.,
Third Floor
Washington, DC 20003

Atomic Industrial Forum
7101 Wisconsin Avenue,
Twelfth Floor
Bethesda, Maryland 20814-
4805

Carnegie Endowment for
International Peace
11 Dupont Circle, N.W.
Washington, DC 20036

Center for Strategic &
International Studies
Georgetown University
1800 K Street, N.W.,
Suite 400
Washington, DC 20006

Committee for National
Security
2000 P Street, N.W.,
Suite 515
Washington, DC 20036

Edison Electric Institute
1111 19th Street, N.W.
Washington, DC 20036

Greenpeace
1611 Connecticut Avenue,
N.W., Third Floor
Washington, DC 20009

Natural Resources Defense
Council, Inc.
1300 New York Avenue,
N.W., Suite 300
Washington, DC 20005

Nuclear Control Institute
1000 Connecticut Avenue,
N.W., Suite 406
Washington, DC 20036

Roosevelt Center for
American Policy Studies
316 Pennsylvania Avenue,
S.E., Suite 500
Washington, DC 20003

United Nations Associa-
tion of the United States
of America
300 East 42nd Street
New York, New York 10017

Westinghouse Electric
Corporation
1801 K Street, N.W.
Washington, DC 20006

Woodrow Wilson Interna-
tional Center for
Scholars
Smithsonian Institution
Building
Washington, DC 20560

INDEX